# Developing Teaching and Learning

The Textbook for the
Cambridge International Certificate
for Teachers and Trainers

Bob Burkill                Ray Eaton

T0349940

CAMBRIDGE
UNIVERSITY PRESS

# CAMBRIDGE
## UNIVERSITY PRESS

University Printing House, Cambridge CB2 8BS, United Kingdom

Cambridge University Press is part of the University of Cambridge.

It furthers the University's mission by disseminating knowledge in the pursuit of education, learning and research at the highest international levels of excellence.

www.cambridge.org
Information on this title: www.cambridge.org/9780521183352

© Cambridge University Press 2011

This publication is in copyright. Subject to statutory exception and to the provisions of relevant collective licensing agreements, no reproduction of any part may take place without the written permission of Cambridge University Press.

First published 2011
20  19  18  17  16  15  14  13  12  11  10 9 8 7 6

Printed in Great Britain by CPI Group (UK) Ltd, Croydon CR0 4YY

*A catalogue for this publication is available from the British Library*

ISBN 978-0-521-18335-2 Paperback

Cambridge University Press has no responsibility for the persistence or accuracy of URLs for external or third-party internet websites referred to in this publication, and does not guarantee that any content on such websites is, or will remain, accurate or appropriate. Information regarding prices, travel timetables, and other factual information given in this work is correct at the time of first printing but Cambridge University Press does not guarantee the accuracy of such information thereafter.

# CONTENTS

# FOREWORD

'It is said that the best teachers are always keen to learn.' This is the first sentence in our syllabus for the Cambridge International Certificate for Teachers and Trainers and expresses a fundamental principle of this popular qualification. This book will certainly be a great help to all teachers who are keen to learn and develop as successful, professional practitioners. As Certificate examiners, Bob Burkill and Ray Eaton are completely in tune with, and expert about the Certificate. They themselves are first-class teachers and trainers, and not least by the definition above. They also are 'keen to learn', in their own teaching practice and as teacher trainers. They are always keen to develop their understanding of teaching and learning and how best to help teachers improve the quality of teaching and learning.

I have been fortunate to witness Bob and Ray leading professional development workshops in many different places and contexts. Their workshops are exciting and inspiring. They have helped many teachers around the world to become more effective and reflective in their design, practice, assessment and evaluation. They have written this book with the same energy, enthusiasm and engagement as they bring to their training. The focus is on improving your practice through applying new ideas and approaches. With Bob and Ray's help in this book, you will enrich your professional thinking and enliven your professional practice.

Dr Paul Beedle
Manager, Professional Development Certification
University of Cambridge International Examinations

# TRIBUTE TO BOB BURKILL

Since the completion of this book Bob Burkill has tragically died. He was the main driving force behind the Cambridge International Certificate for Teachers and Trainers programme and this book is now dedicated to his memory on behalf of his colleagues and all those teachers who have had the joy of working with him to develop teaching and learning across the globe.

*Ray (left) and Bob (right) in Kuwait, relaxing on the waterfront after a busy day training.*

# INTRODUCTION

This book is written for teachers who want to develop the ways in which their learners learn. We hope that it encourages teachers to take their learners on a series of exciting learning journeys and we acknowledge that this will take time, skill and commitment from both learners and teachers. It also requires enterprise and enterprise requires risk – both for the teacher and the learner. We may have great designs but they don't always work out. We need to reflect on what improvement is needed and learn from that to make the next design more effective. It's our belief that the more times you go through these learning cycles as a teacher, the more effective your teaching will be and the richer your learners' experiences will be. Think of it as the gardener does when working to improve the soil.

We owe a great deal of thanks to all the teachers in many different parts of the world who have acted as our learners in our training sessions and have gone on to be trainers themselves. It has been by working with teachers and talking about learning as it happens in their classrooms that many of the sections in this book have been composed. The book is unashamedly practice-based because we can see that the need for developing learning is intrinsic to teachers as well as prompted by outside influences. However, we all reach a point where reflection on practice is not enough. We need to research beyond our own practice to answer some of the complex questions our reflections throw up. With this in mind we have included reference to research and writers where this has been appropriate. We particularly felt that readers should be familiar with at least the basis of learning theories and that is why we have included Section 1 as a piece of essential reading.

The qualification which gave rise to this book, the Cambridge International Certificate for Teachers and Trainers, can be undertaken by practising professional teachers or trainers in any educational culture or context. This book is intended to be similarly generic, though we hope the reader will forgive us if we have referred to teachers and trainers simply as 'teachers'. We hope that those who are preparing themselves to work for the Certificate will find the contents of direct use for their studies, and we hope that those who are not will still find it interesting and stimulating.

Both authors have a habit of wearing red shoes. Not just because the majority of men's shoes are either black or brown and are therefore very boring but because we like to be a bit different, a bit challenging and unafraid of seeming to be so. We hope our readers will 'wear red shoes' professionally by trying to develop learning wisely, enthusiastically and creatively. As practitioners ourselves we are great believers in reflective practice and would encourage readers to design evaluation into their Learning Programmes and Learning Sessions. We are also believers in taking risks with our teaching methods and we encourage our learners to push out the edges of their learning envelopes too. This is very much in the spirit of the Certificate and we have found that most teachers are willing to seize opportunities to develop their practice such that learners can advance the ways in which they learn.

We have set out the book in what we hope is a logical and easily accessible form. Section 1 is about learning itself. We feel that understanding how learning takes place is at the very heart of this work and readers might like to refresh their knowledge of different learning theories before venturing into the more practice-based sections which follow. Section 2 looks at the key ideas which underpin the Certificate. Here we look at reflective practice and call upon research as and when appropriate. These ideas range from macro-scale impacts on education to technical matters such as assessment and evaluation. Our aim here is to relate change to professional practice through innovation and reflection. Sections 3 and 4 bring the reader into more practice based considerations still – the whole business of working with Observers and Trainers and the processes involved in developing an Activity. Section 5 is intended to give you ideas in developing the three Certificate Units.

Whether you are intending to take the Certificate or not we hope that what we have to say will help you to reflect upon your own practice and think about ways forward for your learners. Who knows maybe you will go out there and wear red shoes – metaphorically at least!

*Bob and Ray*

# ACKNOWLEDGEMENT

Paul Beedle at Cambridge International Examinations who has been our guide and inspiration throughout.

Elkie Wootton of CIE who transformed our tousled manuscript into an altogether more professional looking document.

Keeley Laycock, our 'critical friend', whose linguistic skills and careful reading refined and improved our text.

Matthew Meadows for his help with ideas connected to primary education.

Fiona Beedle for her help with the imagination and creativity section.

The team at Cambridge University Press India Private Limited for their friendly professionalism and assistance with production.

# SECTION 1

## INTRODUCTION TO THEORY AND PRACTICE

# DEVELOPING TEACHING AND LEARNING IN A CHANGING WORLD

We have all read articles and books on the relationship of developments in global society and economy to the world of education. These are frequently expressed in grandiose terms and include desires and even targets for educational expansion and achievement 'to meet the needs of these new global developments'. This is all well and good but a long way from helping your second year Maths students next Tuesday! Or is it?

We thought we would begin this section with a bit of reflection on our own experience as qualification designers, trainers and examiners across the world. What have been our own findings as expressed to us by practising teachers whose company we have enjoyed and whose work we have been privileged to observe and assess? Perhaps we can make sense of these macro scale forces at a micro-scale which we can use to benefit our learners.

In bringing these impacts to local learning situations we would like to share five sets of ideas which you might like to think about in the context of your own work. These are drawn from discussions with teachers from a large variety of learning contexts in countries as diverse as Egypt, India, China, Spain, Vietnam, the USA and Singapore.

## A COMMON AWARENESS

Our evidence, though anecdotal, is at least widespread and we have found wherever we go that there is a shared awareness amongst teachers not only of the need for educational change but also that the learners and the learning process are at the heart of their concern. Of course some feel the need to take on board new ways of learning more than others. The overwhelming impression we have gained is one of constructive concern rooted in a notion that the old 'top-down', didactic methods of teaching are no longer suited to most of the needs of twenty first century learners. The implementation of change may be difficult for some teachers for a whole basketful of reasons, but we are always reminded of the need for development by Alvin Toffler's words:

*'The illiterate of the twenty-first century will not be those who cannot read and write but those who cannot learn, unlearn and relearn.'*

## EXTERNAL DRIVERS OF CHANGE

The need for change arises not only from the shared perceptions of practising teachers (*intrinsic* motivation, if you like). It may arise from sources which we identify as *external drivers* – *external* because they are from beyond the teaching-learning context and *drivers* because they are indeed forcing the pace of change. These include:

- government, regional and local initiatives to promote and sustain change
- employer needs and associated support and sponsorship
- international bodies such as UNICEF and CIE
- parental awareness and demands.

Washing around these in ceaseless tides and eddies are changes in access to knowledge and ideas which were almost unforeseen a generation ago. These have done away with the notions that the teacher is the sole gatekeeper of knowledge, that learning occurs only within the walls of educational premises and that education itself will cease at some formally recognised point in an individual's life. Realities such as the information highway, e-learning and lifelong learning will continue to impact upon the reality of learning and we as teachers are well aware of this.

## LEARNERS AS AGENTS OF CHANGE

Missing from the above list of 'drivers' is possibly the most significant, yet uncelebrated agent of change – the learners themselves. As individuals we have always learnt from agencies beyond the classroom – parents, siblings, peers, religious and other cultural organizations – but these tended to reinforce traditional knowledge and values. They were part of an existing learning landscape rather than builders of new learning landscapes. Learners are increasingly plugged in to the Internet and other media opportunities that have quickly exploited the interactive aspect of learning which sits uncomfortably alongside traditional didactic methods. Learners find these new learning landscapes challenging, enjoyable and sometimes even addictive. They must impact on learner perception of what goes on at school. As teachers we need a reality check on our responses to these changes and, in particular:

1. **The impact of mass communications media**

   Movies, newspapers, magazines and books have been overtaken by DVDs, television and radio, the availability of which have been expanded by satellite and cable such that even remote parts of the world can follow news, world soccer and soap operas and the information, understanding and values that go with them. There are even clockwork radios if you are without electricity! Television is an extremely powerful medium and our learners have probably grown up with it. As teachers we have made some use of video and TV clips, mainly as case study, stimulation or explanatory material.

2. **The Internet**

   In less than a generation the Internet has revolutionised our access to information and services. Young people have been especially responsive (and creative) in their use of the world wide web. Blogging and sites such as YouTube and Facebook have produced fascinating dimensions of our 'cyberlives'. This area is less well explored by most adults, teachers included, though as younger e-savvy teachers emerge, this will change. Notice too, that the Internet is interactive.

3. **Mobile telephones**

   Largely unexplored territory as a learning tool but all that may be about to change as media companies explore the boundaries of the phone envelope. The development of technology, like the iPhone, may make learning, even – or especially – interactive learning, mobile. Already the mobile phone is the 'must have' communication machine for many of our learners, and, as technology becomes cheaper internet access will become much more mobile.

## IMPLICATIONS FOR TEACHERS

Even superficial consideration of the above raises important issues for teachers and learners.

- Learners will likely have operative skills well in advance of all but the youngest teachers – such as keyboarding skills, texting and use of search engines.
- Learner access to machines such as iPhones and laptops will vary according to status and financial means.
- Learners see these machines as fashion goods and are highly aware of technological advances and pressurise/stimulate such change, for example, in the electronic games world.
- Learners may well develop new languages of communication – text on mobile phones is a good example.
- These developments are NOT going to be de-invented! Teachers are going to have to:
  - ➤ master at least some of the skills involved in new communication technologies
  - ➤ be aware of technological advances in the pipeline to enhance their own teaching and learning practice
  - ➤ be able to use some of these new capabilities constructively and not just in classes labelled 'ICT' or something similar
  - ➤ join in some of the learners' eagerness to use new techniques
  - ➤ be able to advise on the judicious USE of new techniques especially websites and the dangers of plagiarism.
- There are immense possibilities for developing new learning techniques, especially in creative projects.
- Material downloaded from websites can help teachers share in world wide advances in learning techniques. IGCSE teachers can download past examination questions and other interesting material from the CIE website, for example.
- The message here is to be creative! E-teams of teachers will be able to share reflections and techniques and link with learner chat rooms to gain learner feedback or allow the use of podcasts.

## INITIATING CHANGE

As trainers ourselves we appreciate the difficulties which changing social, economic and technological conditions can set up for teaching and learning. We need to use our own professional teaching skills and the perspective they bring to introduce change effectively. We advocate the use of Active Learning because it is flexible, responsive to varying learner needs and has been shown to be effective. However, the accurate framing of tasks and monitoring of learning environments calls for the use of familiar teaching skills of instruction and discipline. Furthermore Active Learning can only be part of a learning programme as there needs to be space for formative and summative assessment, learner feedback and other forms of learning such as independent learning, private study and research – it is really a case of 'ingenious evolution.'

We have been able to see things through the eyes of our own learners only by talking to them, listening to their ideas and building on these. Any teacher anywhere can do this. We need to build this dialogue with our learners and 'get them on board'. It will give us the fertile ground for experiment – and why not be honest with learners and say to them: 'We are going to try something different, let's try it out and then evaluate it together.'

For many teachers, however, the question is not whether to implement change but 'what kind of change?' and 'how?'. It was to answer those questions (amongst others) that we designed the Cambridge International Certificate for Teachers and Trainers. This challenges teachers to take three new ways forward:

- develop new approaches to teaching
- facilitate Active Learning
- develop one's reflective practice and work more effectively as a professional teacher.

This gives you a useful starting point in developing your learners' learning and your own professional practice, but first we need to refresh our understanding of learning theories and how they underpin our professional practice.

## LEARNING THEORY AND PRACTICE

Many teachers challenge why they need to understand theories of learning, which in their opinion are often abstract and not related to the skills needed to develop good classroom practice. However, understanding the relationship between theory and practice can help teachers to reflect upon and improve their professional practice. This is because, as with any profession, theory is something that is embedded and underpins all good practice.

### INTEGRATING THEORY AND PRACTICE THROUGH REFLECTIVE PRACTICE

Since much of what we learn is from experience, one way of integrating theory and practice is through the systematic and critical reflection of that practice. This perspective is associated with the work of Schön (1983) who suggests that at the heart of all professional practice there is a process of reflection rather than a mechanical application of 'theory'. The professional is someone who is continuously developing her/his underpinning knowledge through reflection of her/his own and others' practice. Therefore this kind of learning is neither wholly theoretical nor wholly practical and knowledge is deepened through the use of the skills themselves.

### THEORIES OF LEARNING AND PROFESSIONAL PRACTICE

When it comes to teaching and learning most teachers think they can recognise 'best practice' without any difficulty. But is this correct? Coffield (2008) says that the one sure way of bringing a conversation to a dead stop is to ask any teacher: 'What's your theory of learning and how does it help to improve your practice?' He argues that teachers do need a theory (or theories) of learning to guide their practice and questions how long we can continue to extol the wonders of learning if we do not even have a definition or description of the term that most can subscribe.

However, learning theory is a huge field of study that is under-developed and full of division and uncertainty. This is because learning is a complex process and no two people learn in the same way. Much of what is learnt in terms of knowledge, skills and attitudes is quickly forgotten unless used on a regular basis. So learning has something to do with being able to remember things and perform skills. Take the example of learning to drive a car. At first, like all learning, it is difficult because there are so many things to remember and skills to perform, often all at once. However, with lots of practice and with the support and guidance of a 'teacher' most people do eventually learn how to drive. They also retain most of the learning if they drive on a regular basis but can and do forget some of the learned knowledge and skills if not frequently practised.

But what was it that made us want or need to learn to drive in the first place? Most people agree that motivation also plays a crucial part in the learning process. We learn to drive either as a need, for example to obtain a job as a taxi driver, or as a want, such as wanting to learn how to drive so the family can be taken on regular holidays. Whilst recognising that memory and motivation play crucial parts in the learning process both concepts still don't get to the heart of how people learn.

In the next few pages, we give you a brief overview of key theories of learning and consider how they underpin or affect professional practice.

## THEORIES AND MODELS OF LEARNING

Theories of learning have been evolving for over one hundred years but what we actually know and understand about how the brain works is the equivalent of still thinking the earth is flat! But there are theories or 'models' of learning that can help to inform our professional practice. 'Modelling' is a technique used to simplify complex processes to help our understanding. Classic examples of modelling are the maps people use to navigate their way around big cities using the underground railway system or diagrams illustrating how blood flows round the human body, as illustrated in Figure 1.

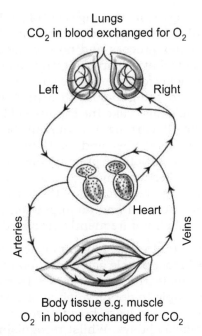

Lungs
$CO_2$ in blood exchanged for $O_2$

Left                Right

Arteries          Heart          Veins

Body tissue e.g. muscle
$O_2$ in blood exchanged for $CO_2$

**Figure 1**: *Model of blood circulation*

## 1. Acquisition model of learning

When teachers and others are asked how they think people learn most come with key features that often amount to nothing more than the transmission and assimilation of knowledge and skills. This aligns closely with what's called the 'acquisition model' of learning which has dominated teaching and learning practice for many years and is illustrated in Figure 2.

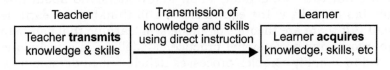

**Figure 2**: *The acquisition model of learning*

The acquisition model views learning as gaining knowledge and skills as the result of using direct instruction techniques such as the teacher giving a presentation, doing a demonstration or getting the learners to watch a DVD. It tends to be a very teacher-led didactic approach where the students, as the receivers of knowledge and skills, are seen as predominantly passive and only learning as the direct result of teaching. This model of learning also tends to encourage what is called surface or rote rather than deep meaningful learning. To illustrate this point consider Figure 3. This is known as 'The Learning Pyramid' and is based on research carried out in the 1960s by The National Training Laboratories (NTL) for Applied Behavioural Science in the USA. The percentages in the diagram represent the average 'retention rate' of information following on from teaching and/or activities by the method indicated.

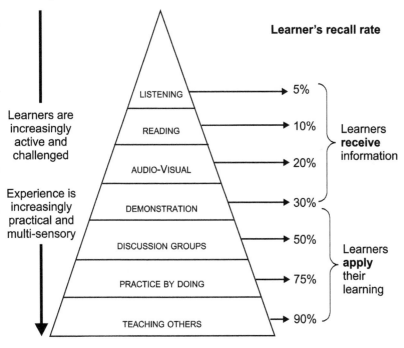

**Figure 3**: *The Learning Pyramid*

This research indicates that if we want our learners to assimilate or gain knowledge and skills that can be recalled or performed as and when required, then using teaching and learning strategies such as listening to a lecture, reading a textbook or watching a video or DVD, are not the best methods to use. Most of the learning is quickly forgotten. Think of a book or magazine article you read one or two weeks ago. How much of it can you actually remember? The research would indicate approximately only 10%. Just listening to somebody talk, like a politician giving a speech, or dare we say it, a teacher giving a lecture, suggests we can only recall approximately 5% of what was said a few days later. After a time lapse of a few months it is likely we would have forgotten nearly everything that was said, unless of course it was truly inspiring. What the research does tell us is that for more effective learning to take place learners need to be participating in activities that make them do, think and then apply their learning. This can be thought of as a participation model of learning and is associated with strategies that promote Active Learning.

2. **Participation model of learning – Kolb's learning cycle**

   A participation model emphasises learning as creating 'meaning' out of experiences. This shifts the focus of learning to being an active rather than a passive process with the teacher acting more as a 'facilitator' of learning rather than just a transmitter of knowledge and skills. Before looking at a participation model of learning let's consider a definition of learning by Abbott (1994) to help draw out some key features:

   *'Learning ... that reflective activity which enables the learner to draw upon previous experience to understand and evaluate the present, so as to shape future action and formulate new knowledge.'*

This definition makes a contrast with the acquisition model as it emphasises that learning is:

- a reflective activity – something to do with thinking
- making connections and creating meanings – linking past

experiences to existing knowledge, skills and understanding, and then relating this to new learning

- trying things out – having reflected about an experience or activity and then making relevant connections, the new learning is then put into practice.

A 'participation model' of learning that emphasises the key concepts of active learning and reflective practice, and is embedded in the Cambridge International Certificate for Teachers and Trainers (CICTT), is Kolb's (1984) learning cycle. This model of learning is illustrated in Figure 4.

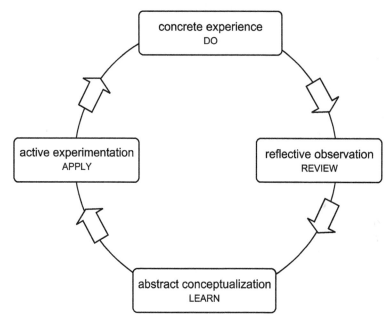

**Figure 4**: *Kolb's learning cycle – a participation model of learning*

So how can an understanding of Kolb's model of learning help to improve a teacher's professional practice? Let's start the learning cycle by considering what Kolb calls a 'concrete experience'. This means the learners must do something. Whilst the 'doing' may involve listening to the teacher, reading a book or watching a DVD, when most people start to think about how they really understood a subject or developed a skill it usually involved more active methods of learning such as taking part in a discussion, visiting a museum, doing a science experiment, etc. Think about learning a new skill such as how to prepare and cook a fish. We could just read a recipe book or observe someone demonstrating how to do it. However, no matter how many times we read the book or observe the demonstration, it won't be as effective as preparing and cooking the fish ourselves, even though initially it might not taste very good!

The next stage of the cycle is reflection, which involves thinking about or reviewing the experience. Just preparing and cooking the fish over and over again does not necessarily mean we will develop our knowledge and skills and become a better cook. To learn we must think about the experience and start to make 'connections' with our existing, present and past experiences. On reflection did we gut and clean the fish properly, was the oven set at too high or low a temperature, was the cooking time too much or too little? Learners need to be given time to think and reflect as it is an important part of the learning process and one to which many teachers often pay insufficient attention to.

Kolb calls the next stage of the cycle 'abstract conceptualisation' and this is what we usually think of as learning. What happens is that we start to make 'connections' between neurons in the brain and in doing so 'construct' our own meanings of this new learning linked to what we already know. This concept of learning is called 'constructivism' and we can observe this

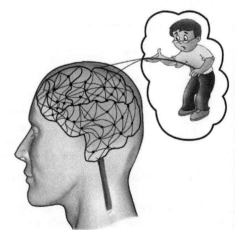

**Figure 5**: *Wiring of the brain*

important part of the learning cycle in our everyday teaching practice. This is because sometimes our learners don't quite make the right links in the creative meaning-making process.

Petty (2009) illustrates this point by looking at genuine mistakes made by children in examinations:

> *'History calls them Romans because they never stayed in one place for very long',* or
>
> *'Large animals are found in the sea because there is nowhere else to put them'* or
>
> *'Beethoven expired in 1827, and later died for this'*

These genuine mistakes show 'meaning making' in practice. If learners remembered everything a teacher told them they would not make these kinds of mistakes, they would either remember or not. Conceptual errors show that people make their own mental constructs; they don't just remember other people's. If you asked 10 people to read a poem they will interpret its meanings in many different ways. What most will not be able to do is repeat the poem word for word on the first time of hearing. We could compare making these connections or 'wiring of the brain' to a telephone engineer wiring up an exchange, it's all about making the right connections. The telephone engineer has colour coded wires to help make the connections; our students also need similar help, most often from a teacher as illustrated in Figure 5. We also need to acknowledge that learning something new is usually hard but once we start to make the right 'connections' it becomes easier the more we do it. Perhaps the first time we cooked the fish it was too dry but on reflection we might make the 'learning connections' that the oven was set too high and the cooking time too long for that type and weight of fish.

In the final part of the cycle, which Kolb calls 'active experimentation', the learner tries out or applies their newly learned knowledge or skill. The next time we cook our fish we will make adjustments to the cooking temperature and time. Even then we might still require further or new concrete experiences to improve our skills and knowledge, and so the cycle continues.

Let us now use Kolb's learning cycle to model our teaching practice and see how it can be used to improve future performance.

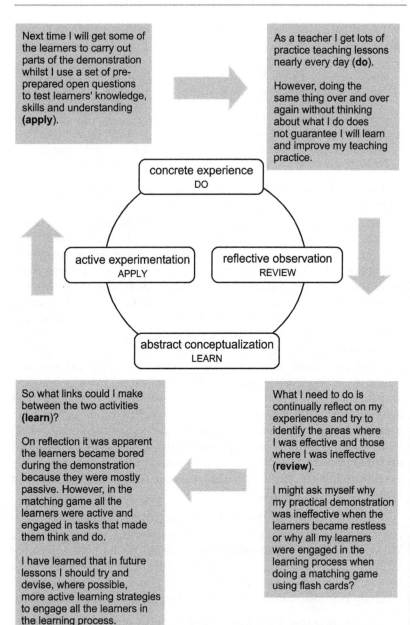

Next time I will get some of the learners to carry out parts of the demonstration whilst I use a set of pre-prepared open questions to test learners' knowledge, skills and understanding (**apply**).

As a teacher I get lots of practice teaching lessons nearly every day (**do**).

However, doing the same thing over and over again without thinking about what I do does not guarantee I will learn and improve my teaching practice.

concrete experience
DO

active experimentation
APPLY

reflective observation
REVIEW

abstract conceptualization
LEARN

So what links could I make between the two activities (**learn**)?

On reflection it was apparent the learners became bored during the demonstration because they were mostly passive. However, in the matching game all the learners were active and engaged in tasks that made them think and do.

I have learned that in future lessons I should try and devise, where possible, more active learning strategies to engage all the learners in the learning process.

What I need to do is continually reflect on my experiences and try to identify the areas where I was effective and those where I was ineffective (**review**).

I might ask myself why my practical demonstration was ineffective when the learners became restless or why all my learners were engaged in the learning process when doing a matching game using flash cards?

**Figure 6**: *Kolb's learning cycle – used as part of reflective practice*

Hopefully the example of applying the theory of Kolb's learning cycle to a teacher's professional practice illustrates how it can help to improve teaching by having a greater understanding of how people learn. However, when considering any theory or 'model' of learning we should always keep an open and enquiring mind as it is not an exact science. The point to be made here is that teachers need to be able to relate their practical experiences to any relevant theory or model of learning, and then learn from it. Clearly there are occasions when teachers, out of necessity, have to give a short lecture or do a demonstration based on the acquisition model of learning. What's important under these circumstances is that they adopt strategies that make the lecture or presentation as lively, interesting and interactive as possible. The use of Information Computer Technology (ICT) that incorporates lots of visuals and relevant video clips can help when using this approach as it helps to keep the learners' attention. What must be avoided is thinking a twenty minute PowerPoint presentation showing bullet point after bullet point is an effective use of ICT – it isn't, just ask your learners.

## TWO COGNITIVE APPROACHES TO LEARNING – BLOOM AND PIAGET

BLOOM'S TAXONOMY

If learners create their own meanings from past and existing experiences it implies that in any class they probably all have a slightly different understanding of any information being received. So what can teachers do to help their learners learn more effectively? Using a cognitive approach based on Bloom's Taxonomy might help practically as it stresses that learning can be classified into three domains or categories. Within each domain there is a hierarchy or spectrum of difficulty and this can be thought of as a 'ladder' of learning. What the teacher needs to do is develop learning materials that move the learners from the low or bottom end of the ladder to the high or top end no matter what their level of ability.

The three domains into which Bloom (1965) classifies all learning into are:

- cognitive – knowledge, knowing (how and why) and thinking skills
- psychomotor – motor skills or physical skills
- affective – feelings, attitudes, emotions and values.

Each of the domains within Bloom's Taxonomy is shown diagrammatically below.

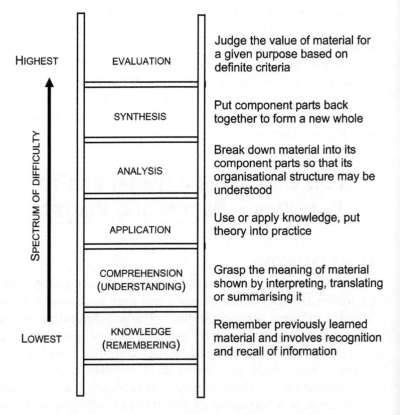

**Figure 7**: *Bloom's Taxonomy in the Cognitive Domain*

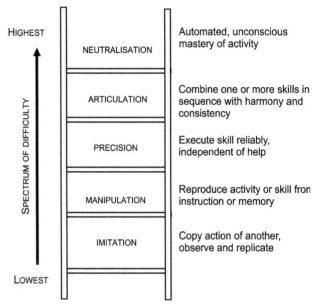

**Figure 8**: *Bloom's Taxonomy in the Psychomotor Domain*

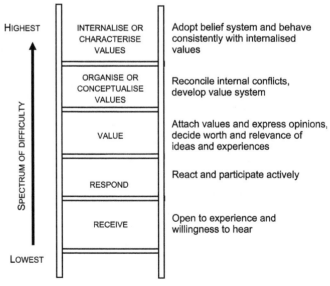

**Figure 9**: *Bloom's Taxonomy in the Affective Domain*

Bloom's Taxonomy in the Cognitive Domain has received the most attention when trying to relate theory to practice. If considered as a spectrum of task difficulty it moves from 'simple' tasks, such as simply recalling knowledge, to much harder tasks such as evaluating an argument. What this means is that we need to design a sequence of activities which enable the weaker learners to experience success and the stronger ones to be 'stretched' or challenged in their learning. This helps to put into context the concept of differentiation, where all the learners are learning at a level comparable to their ability. To ensure this happens the 'harder' activities are often broken down into a series of tasks that enable the weaker learners to progress at their own pace. According to Atherton (2005), teachers ought not to try and address the higher levels of the domain until those below them have been covered.

## DIFFERENTIATED LEARNING

Let us take the example of using a crossword as a group activity to help students learn some relevant knowledge through research. To help create a spectrum of differentiated learning we could design and create four different crosswords.

CROSSWORD 1 The learners are given both the clues and the answers to the clues. The answers would be set out in a random fashion with a few of them containing the same number of letters so the learners can't just match them directly to the clues. Matching the right answers to the clues will help develop the learners' knowledge and skills, and it would be expected that all of them would experience success doing this task. It also means it is not a memory test, which many learners find really difficult.

CROSSWORD 2 The learners are given the clues and the answers. However, this time there will be more answers than clues and some of the 'wrong' answers will act as distracters. This task will develop both knowledge and comprehension and again, all the learners will be expected to achieve this task.

CROSSWORD 3 The learners are only given the clues. Skilfully devised, this crossword could involve knowledge (remembering), comprehension (understanding), application and some analysis within the cognitive domain. It would be expected that the majority, but not necessarily all of the learners, would complete this task.

CROSSWORD 4 The learners are given the answers and they must make up the clues. Completion of this task potentially involves the full spectrum of Bloom's Taxonomy from knowledge recall to evaluation. Not all the learners would be expected to complete this task.

## PIAGET – SCHEMAS AND STAGES OF COGNITIVE LEARNING DEVELOPMENT

Piaget's research formed the basis of constructivist learning theory. He became interested in the mistakes children made and felt their errors offered an insight into the way children perceived logical problems. There was something 'going on' that could not be explained by a lack of ability. He noticed that children were routinely giving the same 'wrong' answers and became interested in why this happened. He concluded that children's 'wrong' answers were not random but followed a logical pattern based on conclusions drawn from their own experiences. He called these conclusions 'schemas' and believed that children are able to adapt them when they have new experiences in one of two ways:

- assimilation – occurs when children realise their schema fits another situation
- accommodation – happens when children realise that their schema does not 'fit' what is happening; this forces the child to develop a new schema based on the latest experience.

Piaget also felt that as well as learning by developing and adapting schemas children also seemed to pass through different stages of cognitive development and each stage appeared to be linked to their biological development as shown in the following table.

PIAGET'S STAGES OF COGNITIVE LEARNING DEVELOPMENT

| STAGE | AGE | OBSERVATIONS – CHILDREN |
| --- | --- | --- |
| SENSORY MOTOR | 0–2 | • learn about the environment from their senses<br>• start to develop the idea that a person or object they cannot see still exists – *object permanence*<br>• learn mainly from trial and error methods |
| PRE-OPERATIONAL | 2–4 | • start to use language to express thoughts and symbols in play<br>• are *egocentric* – see things from their viewpoint only<br>• tend to think that non-living things and animals have the same feelings as them (*animism*) |
| INTUITIVE | 4–7 | • start to think in a classifactory way but may be unaware of classifications<br>• tend to be taken in by how things look and appear |
| CONCRETE OPERATIONS | 7–11 | • can see things from another's point of view – *decentring*<br>• start to reason, less easily fooled by appearances (*conserve*)<br>• can use abstract symbols – eg mathematical signs and writing and are developing complex reasoning skills but they still need physical objects to solve some problems – eg counters |
| FORMAL OPERATIONS | 11–15 | • are able to think in the abstract – this means that they can manipulate ideas in their head such as solving sums<br>• are more logical and methodical when trying to solve a problem – eg not using a trial and error approach |

It is helpful for all teachers, no matter what age group they teach, to think about Piaget's stages of cognitive development and the types of learning activities devised for their students. Piaget suggested that not everyone would move on to the formal operations stage and that play is vital in the learning process of children as it shows their mastery over cognitive problems and forms the basis of their imagination.

It does seem a pity that we tend to move away from the concept of play and active learning in many subject areas as children get older. Go into most classrooms where young people under the age of 6 or 7 are learning and like Piaget, observe and reflect on what is happening. Is this very different to a class of mixed ability of 15 to 16-year-olds in a school or college? Why is it we arrange the classrooms differently and use more didactic teaching methods rather than focus on devising activities that allow the learners to 'play' using teaching and learning strategies such as role play and the use of matching games? All learning theories are open to debate and challenge and Piaget's are no different, but they can help us to understand more fully how children learn and to structure activities to meet their needs.

*Mariam, I can't believe Issy, at only five years of age, can programme the DVD player after playing with it for only five minutes and you spent over two hours reading and following instructions from the manual and still failed to get it to work!*

## ADULT LEARNING – KNOWLES' ANDRAGOGY

Teachers are usually familiar with the term pedagogy which can be defined as 'the science of teaching' and is usually associated with teaching children rather than adults. Fairly recently the term andragogy, which can be defined as 'the science and art of helping adults to learn' has come more to our attention through the work of Malcolm Knowles.

Knowles (1984) argues that adults learn differently to children and he developed an andragogical model of learning based on five assumptions about the characteristics of adult learners that are different from assumptions made about child learners.

The five assumptions made by Knowles can be summarised as follows:

- self-concept – adults move from being a dependent learner towards being a 'self-directed learner'
- experience – adult learners have a variety of life experiences that are a rich resource for learning
- readiness to learn – adults are ready to learn those things they need to know to cope effectively with life situations
- orientation to learning – adults are motivated to learn to the extent that they perceive it will help them perform tasks they confront in life situations, accordingly their orientation towards learning shifts from one of subject-centeredness to problem-centeredness
- motivation to learn – adult learners need to know why they need to learn something before undertaking to learn it and the motivation to learn is internal.

The following table is a useful comparison of the main differences between pedagogy and andragogy based on Knowles' five assumptions.

| ASSUMPTION | PEDAGOGICAL APPROACH | ANDRAGOGICAL APPROACH |
| --- | --- | --- |
| • concept of the learner | dependent personality | increasingly self-directed |
| • role of the learner's experience | to be built on rather than used as a resource | a rich resource for learning by self and others |
| • readiness to learn | uniform by age, level and curriculum | develops from life tasks and problems |
| • orientation to learning | subject-centred | task or problem-centred |
| • motivation to learn | by external rewards and punishment | by internal incentives and curiosity |

So how does Knowles' theory of andragogy impact on our teaching practice bearing in mind we normally consider adult learners as being aged 16 plus. This really centres on the types of learning activities we are able to devise for 'adult' learners and how they approach them. The following guidelines will help to put some of this learning theory into practice.

- Share the session learning objectives with the learners and then, when appropriate, negotiate how they might achieve them. This involves the learners in the design process where they accept a share of the responsibility for planning, implementing and evaluating the course. This is an example of what Knowles means when he talks about adult learners becoming increasingly self-directed and not so dependent on the teacher.
- Devise activities that utilize the learners' existing knowledge, skills and understanding as they bring to each lesson a wealth of different experiences. This is an example of using the learners as a rich resource for learning.
- Devise differentiated activities that are meaningful to the learners and where they are encouraged to provide peer support to facilitate the learning of others by reflecting upon their own experiences. This encourages the learners' readiness to learn through activities developed from life tasks and problems.

- Activities should be devised with an emphasis on tackling problems and developing skills based on the learners' present integrated practice. This makes the orientation to learning more task or problem-centred rather than subject-centred.
- As the course progresses, activities are devised where the learners take more responsibility for their learning and become less dependent on the teacher. This helps them to accept that learning is an internal process and not something the teacher 'does' to them. The motivation to learn is intrinsic rather than extrinsic.

*We are fortunate class that this evening we can call upon Brian's experience as a former bank robber to tell us about the problems of using oxy-acetylene welding cutting equipment in confined spaces.*

## LEARNING AND MOTIVATION – MASLOW'S HIERARCHY OF NEEDS

The common perception is that a motivated person can learn better than someone who is unmotivated and one of the main challenges any teacher faces is to encourage a learner who doesn't want to learn to engage in the learning process. The most well known theory of motivation is Maslow's (1987) *hierarchy of needs* and how this can be related to our everyday teaching practice is illustrated in Figure 10.

**Theory** / **Practice**

**Self Actualisation** – realising personal potential
Be enthusaistic, supportive and promote optimism, encourage projects and innovative ideas/ experimentation. Be positive about the future.

**Esteem needs** – self esteem, achievement, respect for others
Treat learner with dignity. Encourage independence, welcome ideas. Praise when appropriate and guide as necessary.

**Belonging, love and acceptance needs** – work group, family, affection
Show respect, and that you care. Promote interaction between learners and a cohesive class climate.

**Safety needs** – protection from the elements, security, order, law, limits, stability
Maintain confidentiality/privacy. Treat learners fairly and equally. Follow safety procedures.

**Psychological needs** – fresh air, food, drink, shelter, warmth, sleep
Ensure room is warm, ventilated, seating is comfortable. Provide adequate breaks. Arrange furniture according to needs.

**Figure 10**: *Maslow's hierarchy of needs*

Whilst Maslow's hierarchy of needs assists us in explaining the conditions that motivate students to get ready to learn, and many teachers think this is fairly self-evident, it stops at precisely the point we need most help. How do we motivate a student who doesn't want to learn? Perhaps the most commonly used technique, and one familiar to us all, is based on the conditioning of behaviour using a system of 'rewards' and 'punishments'. This is often referred to as the 'carrot and stick approach' and is associated with 'extrinsic' motivation or the need to learn. Some examples of the reasons teachers give to students for needing to learn are:

- if you don't pass your exams and go to university you will end up doing a boring poorly paid job with no future
- if you complete all today's tasks you won't have to do them for homework

- you have the potential to be as good as your sister/brother/ friend but your lack of application will result in you being the class failure
- you will disappoint your parents with your poor attitude and lack of academic progress
- if you don't gain this qualification your chances of the job promotion you so dearly want will not happen.

The problem we have with relying solely on a carrot and stick approach, and with really challenging students it tends to be more stick than carrot, is that if the strategy doesn't work what do we do next? That's why strategies used to motivate learners adopting this approach should be treated with caution.

Ideally we want our learners to be intrinsically motivated such that they want, rather than need, to learn. Often this can be achieved by making the learning as active, challenging and meaningful as possible. For example, in mathematics many learners struggle with the concept that you must multiply and divide numbers before adding or subtracting them. Many teachers teach this concept by initially asking learners to solve a sum such as 2 + 3 x 4. Most learners give the answer as 20 when in fact it is 14. If the concept is taught in a more 'meaningful' context, such as shopping for clothes, the teacher could use role play and get the learners to go 'shopping' and purchase 2 jackets and 3 packs of shirts, where each pack contains 4 shirts. When using this approach most learners arrive at the correct answer of 14 when asked how many items of clothing have been purchased. We are certain you could think of examples in your teaching area where similar strategies to motivate your learners to learn could be adopted.

Young learners tend to be more intrinsically motivated through play and their natural curiosity with what's going on around them. Problems tend to arise when the pressure of working towards external examinations comes about and the learners ask questions like 'Why do I have to learn to divide two fractions when I can't see when I am going to use this skill in real life?', or 'What's the point of drawing and labelling the digestive system of a rat when I'm going to be a sales executive?'. On the other hand adult learners find learning really motivating when they can see practical applications for their new knowledge and skills and respond positively to tasks related to their everyday experience based on real life situations. The concept of extrinsic and intrinsic motivation is illustrated in the following diagram.

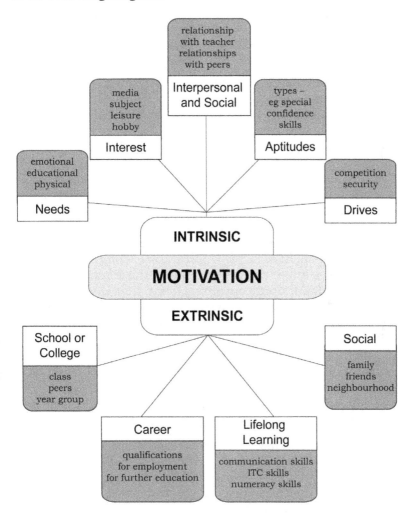

**Figure 11**: *Expanding motivational themes*

To be a more effective teacher we need to design learning activities which encourage students to learn using some of the motivational agents identified in Figure 11. A truly inspirational teacher may be very aware of these agents within her/his learners and be able to capture and harness their imagination in a remarkable way. Such individuals are rare and can vary in their effectiveness. Yet most teachers can learn from their success and be motivationally effective by considering a few important ideas.

- Devise and develop learning activities which engage with learner interests, needs and aspirations. This involves a degree of empathy with your learners and the worlds they come from and aspire to.
- Learners are drawn towards innovation. Try a new teaching/ learning method and invite the learners to join you in the experiment. This 'bonds' teachers and learners and produces rich learner feedback and a positive learning environment.
- Without being in any way 'forced' or 'over the top' showing your own enthusiasm is likely to be something of a motivator in itself. Use positive language and body language.
- Encouragement is a big motivational factor although it is not always linked to success. Indeed it is often said that it is actually 'failure plus encouragement' that leads to success. Remember, everyone thrives on encouragement.
- Vary the contents of your learning programme. Many teachers still monopolise many sessions with lots of 'teacher talk' and the only activities required of the learners is to listen and copy notes from a screen or whiteboard; this is not motivational.
- It may be that your learning programme is defined externally, but how you teach it is not.

Use of external motivational factors, such as 'doing well in the exams', needs very careful handling. It might wake up some individuals but put others under quite intolerable pressure. Increasingly, instead of teaching to exams, there is more of an emphasis on equipping learners with the knowledge, skills and understanding they need for life-long learning and to compete in a technologically advanced world. Figure 12 illustrates some ideas on using extrinsic motivation.

# IDEAS FOR USING EXTRINSIC MOTIVATION

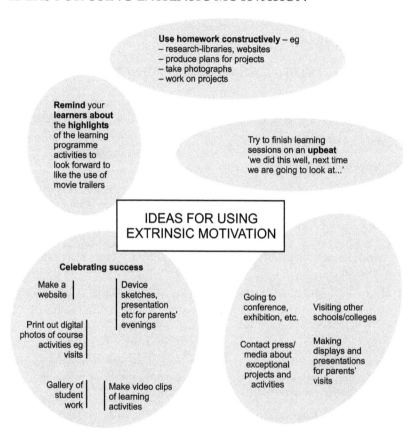

**Use homework constructively** – eg
– research-libraries, websites
– produce plans for projects
– take photographs
– work on projects

**Remind** your **learners about** the **highlights** of the learning programme activities to look forward to like the use of movie trailers

Try to finish learning sessions on an **upbeat** 'we did this well, next time we are going to look at...'

**IDEAS FOR USING EXTRINSIC MOTIVATION**

Celebrating success

Make a website

Print out digital photos of course activities eg visits

Gallery of student work

Device sketches, presentation etc for parents' evenings

Make video clips of learning activities

Going to conference, exhibition, etc.

Visiting other schools/colleges

Contact press/ media about exceptional projects and activities

Making displays and presentations for parents' visits

**Figure 12**: *Making use of extrinsic motivation*

**Activity**
Take any one of the shaded areas on the diagram above and work out how you can use its ideas (and any you may have) to make extrinsic motivation benefit learners' work and activities in your learning sessions and learning experience.

Finally it needs emphasising that a learner's failure to learn is often due to a teacher's failure to motivate. Clearly a vital role of the teacher is to understand the many factors that determine whether students are motivated, or not, to learn. The following table attempts to identify some elements of professional practice that can act as motivators or de-motivators in the classroom.

MOTIVATORS VERSUS DE-MOTIVATORS

| MOTIVATORS | DE-MOTIVATORS |
|---|---|
| • enthusiastic teacher using a variety of teaching and learning strategies | • didactic teacher who mainly talks at or lectures the students |
| • active learning tasks with lots of learner involvement | • passive learning tasks with little or no learner involvement |
| • learning tasks are meaningful and relate to previous learning | • learning tasks are obscure and do not relate to previous learning |
| • learning activities set at the right levels and differentiated so all learners experience some success | • learning activities not differentiated and too hard at the beginning or do not stretch the more able learners |
| • variety of teaching and learning methods used – lessons unpredictable | • lack of variety of teaching and learning methods – lessons predictable |
| • changes of lesson pace with learners given 'thinking time' | • pace of lesson too fast/ slow and learners not given 'thinking' time' |
| • learners given individual support | • waiting for help from teacher |
| • lots of praise and positive body language from teacher | • no praise and negative body language from teacher |
| • timely feedback from formative tests | • no feedback from formative tests |
| • learners know lesson content and what is expected of them | • learners unsure of lesson content and what is expected of them |

*Kevin Lee, if you were as motivated to actually do your homework as you are in thinking up excuses why you haven't, we wouldn't be having this conversation.*

## LEARNING AND MEMORY

We think much of what we learn has a lot to do with having a good memory. However, we need to be aware that the process known as memory involves both remembering and forgetting. In any one academic year at school or at college we expect learners to remember and learn an awful lot of knowledge and skills content. It has been compared to taking a 200 mile train journey and remembering everything observed when looking out from the carriage window!

The human memory system is very complex and not fully understood. To help our understanding let's use another 'model' of learning this time based on Broadbent's (1958) filter theory of selective attention which is shown in Figure 13.

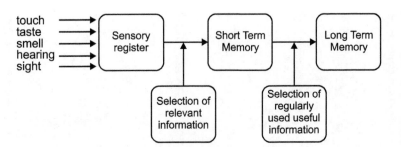

**Figure 13**: *Simplified version of Broadbent's model of memory*

*I'm disappointed that nobody in the class remembered that today is my birthday after I reminded you all yesterday.*

What the model tells us is that the sensory register in the brain filters out most of the information being received before it even reaches our short term memory on the basis of whether we think it is relevant or not. Even when information does pass into the short term memory, after a very short time we forget most of it if not used on a regular basis.

For information to pass into the long term memory, the short term memory must process and structure it so that it makes sense. This means new information should be related to previous experiences. It is also important that the brain is not overloaded with too much information at any one time and is given time to process it. You may have experienced the situation where, being lost in a town or city, you have stopped to ask for directions to a particular place. If the person gives you a lot of information it is more than likely that after a few minutes you will have forgotten what has been said and have to ask again. This is because most people's short-term memory has the capacity of only storing between 5 and 9 separate 'chunks' of information at any one time (try the memory test in Appendix 1 and see how many 'chunks' of information you can remember).

Even after passing into the long term memory information will eventually be forgotten unless used or recalled on a regular basis. We can all think of an examination we passed with flying colours years ago but, if faced with the same test today, we would probably struggle to pass. So why should we expect students to remember things studied months ago without continually revisiting them? Whilst some students can pass examinations by doing last minute revision it tends to be rote learning and is quickly forgotten.

Teachers should keep in mind their own experiences concerning students who seem to remember easily and those who forget quickly. How many times have you heard a teacher say: 'I did a one hour presentation on this topic only two days ago and today they can barely remember a thing'? But let's think about this from a learner's perspective as they get equally frustrated and disheartened when they can't recall information. If they have to listen to a one hour presentation of predominantly 'teacher talk' then, as Petty (2004: p. 155) explains, at an average of 200 words per minute, the students could be listening to up to 12000 words, typically the number in a short book! Is it any wonder they retain very little of the information?

Clearly memory plays an important part in the learning process and it's the teacher's responsibility to plan learning activities that will help learners retain information in the long term memory. Using our existing knowledge and understanding of learning, and particularly constructivism, as teachers we can do the following to help our students remember (learn) and then recall information:

1. **Construct meaning through active learning**
   A student is more likely to remember what they have learnt about Newton's Laws of Gravity if they drop objects of different mass from the same height and see which ones hit the ground first and decide the outcomes rather than reading what happens from a book.

2. **Connect to prior knowledge so new learning can be associated with existing understanding**
   A difficult concept such as electricity can be compared to the flow of water running in a stream.

3. **Engage the emotions to strengthen the neural connections**
   In a science class if the students are allowed to smell a noxious gas or feel a pulse before and after exercise then their emotions are more likely to be heightened. The emotional content of a lesson can also be increased through the use of humour, creating anticipation, or through reading or watching significant triumphs, disasters, historical events, etc.

'... and that ends today's lesson on the importance of the rainforest on the world's eco-system.'

4. **Present learning in context so the brain makes more associations and constructs more meaning**

   Students often learn far more from an educational visit to a zoo, power station, hospital, etc, as it is more memorable than just discussing it in a classroom setting or seeing it on a TV screen.

5. **Make the learning relevant as the brain is selective about the information it transfers to the long term memory**

   Role playing by writing a letter of application for a job to develop literacy skills or using a foreign language to order a meal in a restaurant to develop language skills is relevant to what people do in everyday life.

6. **Use learning activities that are multi-sensory as we remember most of what we hear, read, see, say and do**

   Lessons should contain regular changes of activities to engage as many of the senses as possible.

7. **Present learning in short bursts as we tend to remember far more information at the start and finish of presentations rather than the middle**

   Changes of activities and variation of pace help to achieve this so in effect there are lots of mini starts and finishes. The introduction to the lesson should also link back to previous learning and the conclusion should recap what has been learnt.

8. **Regularly review learning as most information is forgotten after a very short time**

   The use of short quizzes, crosswords, games, etc, can be used to re-visit learning and are also fun. This reinforcement of learning is very important.

9. **Devising activities that engage both hemispheres of the brain**

   Most people find it easier to remember the words of a song than the words of a poem because singing stimulates both the left and right sides of the brain. The left or analytical side of the brain works in a very sequential way, from the parts to the whole and oversees language, logic and number concepts. The right or global side of the brain is non-verbal and intuitive, working from the whole to the parts and deals with visualisation, imagination, music, art, rhyme and rhythm. So why don't we use group singing as a learning strategy more often with all learners, no matter what their age? Try it – as most learners, even the shy ones, love to sing. Most of us have learnt essential knowledge such as the alphabet or our multiplication tables by singing them out loud. It also gives you and your students the opportunity to be creative by composing songs that will help them remember and learn.

10. **Employ memory strategies such as the use of mnemonics (rhymes, rules, phrases, diagrams, acronyms, etc)**
    To help with spelling in the English language we may have learnt the simple rhyme 'i before e except after c' or in music lessons the order of notes on staves of music on the line as EGBDF (Every Good Boy Deserves Favour) and the notes between the lines as FACE even though we can't play a musical instrument!

## TEACHING AND LEARNING

It is important to recognise that teaching and learning are not two distinct activities but intertwined elements of a single reciprocal process, or if you like, the two sides of one coin. The more teachers seek to understand how people learn and improve their teaching practice, the better able they are to facilitate effective learning. But how do we judge what is effective learning? One way of doing this is to consider the different types of 'interventions' that have an impact on learner attainment or achievement. Extensive research carried out by Hattie (1999) did just this and the 'interventions' found to have the biggest impact on learner achievement are:

1. **Active learning**
   This means students practise important skills and apply new knowledge. During the lesson the teacher will:
   ➢ review previous learning
   ➢ explain, demonstrate and think out loud

> ➢ continually check the learning of groups and individuals in terms of what they are doing and how they are doing it
> ➢ conclude by reviewing what has been learned.

## 2. Feedback

Research carried out by Black and Wiliam (1998) concurs with Hattie that feedback, closely linked to formative assessment, has a major impact on effective learning. One way of putting this into practice is to use what Petty (2004: pp. 65-67) calls a 'Medals and Missions' approach. A 'Medal' is feedback that informs the learner what they have done well such as '*Your interpretation of the poem was insightful and well written*'. It is important to remember that grades and marks are measurements not Medals.

A 'Mission' is feedback to the student about what they need to improve, correct, or work on. It is best when it is forward looking and positive such as '*Use paragraphs to make your well argued critique easier to read*'. Again, measurements such as grades do not usually give this information.

## 3. Reinforcement

As teachers we can give reinforcement of learning to our learners in many different ways such as:
> ➢ re-visiting topics on a regular basis
> ➢ listening and accepting all their ideas with respect so that they are not afraid to ask questions when they don't understand
> ➢ acknowledging them as individuals who have unique thoughts
> ➢ showing interest and continually praising their work
> ➢ spending time with them on a 1:1 or small group basis
> ➢ using positive body language such as smiling or nodding.

## 4. Quality of teaching

In too many lessons it is the teacher who does most of the talking and consequently most of the learning! This is because they think learners learn best by being lectured or talked at. Their thinking is based on what is known as 'folk psychology' and how they were taught. They learnt in this way so it must be alright! However, as we have tried to demonstrate throughout this section, most research evidence clearly indicates otherwise. If teachers are to improve their professional practice and facilitate active learning then having some insight into learning theories will help them do this. In doing so they should start to move away from using 'top down' authoritarian didactic approaches. This will improve the quality of their teaching and the learners' learning experiences. Some of the active learning methods teachers adopt for their learners within a learning programme include:

- ➢ practical/group work
- ➢ use of ICT/audio visual
- ➢ educational visit
- ➢ role play/simulation
- ➢ discussion or debate
- ➢ visiting speaker
- ➢ project work
- ➢ pair work
- ➢ peer assessment/self assessment
- ➢ learner interactive presentations
- ➢ scaffolding.

Most teachers are familiar with the active learning methods mentioned above but perhaps a method that does need some further explanation is scaffolding.

## SCAFFOLDING LEARNING

### BRUNER AND VYGOTSKY

The term 'scaffolding' is a metaphor to describe techniques teachers use to provide different types and levels of support to meet a learner's individual learning needs. The basic concept, which was developed by the psychologist Jerome Bruner and based on the work of Lev Vygotsky, is that when a learner is learning new or difficult tasks they are given lots of assistance, usually, but not always, provided by the teacher. As the learner begins to demonstrate mastery of the new learning the levels of support or 'scaffolds' are gradually withdrawn to shift the responsibility for learning from the teacher to the learner.

For example, a young child needs a lot of support when learning a new skill such as reading. At first the teacher provides this support by devising a range of activities or tasks that develops the child's ability to recognise the shapes and sounds of letters and then words. After a suitable period of time the teacher then removes some of the 'scaffolding' or support as the child begins to read sentences. Eventually, all the scaffolding is removed when the child can read successfully without support.

The common day-to-day techniques we use to scaffold learning, often without consciously thinking about it, include the use of:

- cues, prompts, hints, partial solutions, think-aloud modelling and direct instruction
- directed open questioning to help learners solve a problem or complete a task
- activities that involve peer support or tutoring where learners help each other in small group settings with teacher assistance only when required.

Scaffolding is a powerful teaching and learning technique that requires a great deal of skill to use effectively. However, it needs to be acknowledged that teaching large classes, often with restraints on both time and resources, makes devising a suitable range of 'scaffolded' activities, at different levels, to meet the needs of all learners, virtually impossible. However, when skilfully devised scaffolded activities have the potential to engage all the learners in the lesson and help them progress. Instead of passively listening to presented information they are prompted by the teacher to build on their existing knowledge and understanding to develop new learning. In working with learners who have low self-esteem and learning difficulties it provides an opportunity to give them some positive feedback, which in turn helps to motivate them to learn. Another advantage of scaffolding is that it can minimize the level of frustration of the learner. This is extremely important with students who have learning difficulties as they can easily become frustrated, shut down and refuse to participate in further learning during that particular lesson.

Vygotsky also emphasises the importance of play in the learning process particularly during learning in the early years and in groups as it enables learners to go beyond what he calls the 'zone of proximal development' or ZPD in their learning. When learners are learning with others rather than alone they have available the emotional and intellectual support that often allows them to go beyond their present levels of knowledge and skills. But does this happen just with young children? Think of occasions when you have been surprised by how much you have learnt from the support of other members in a group. It happens frequently, no matter what your age, and emphasizes the importance of active learning in groups. The role of the teacher is also important in helping learners to perform beyond what they think they can achieve.

*I'm not sure my teaching colleague explained the techniques of scaffolding correctly when we discussed different ways of doing it in our little chat yesterday.*

# SECTION 2

# KEY IDEAS IN THE CERTIFICATE

## PLANNING AND DESIGN IN TEACHING AND LEARNING

## THE IDEA OF DESIGN

The idea of living in a world which we have designed rather than one which was 'traditional' and inherited from past generations has gained ground over the last one hundred years. We are becoming used to designed environments such as houses, suburbs, even whole cities. Most of us see the fruits of design around us – designer clothes, shoes and perfumes. In fact almost every manufactured good is created through design processes. Designer brands then market these goods and services and we identify price, quality and style through names such as Jimmy Choo, Prada, Levi's, Marriott and BMW.

Yet not many people think of the teacher as a designer. Perhaps this is because when we were at school ourselves we only saw teachers working in the classroom. As practising teachers we know that a large proportion of our work exists beyond where we actually teach. Part of that work falls into the 'design' category. Think for a moment about what you actually design: Learning Programmes and Learning Sessions spring to mind immediately. They are of great concern to us but they are not the only design work we engage in as teachers. Look at Figure 14 and see if you can add any design activities which you carry out.

Design in the broader, in the more commercial sense, usually arises from consumer needs and aspirations and is, for the designer, initiated by a formalisation of needs into a design brief or specification. This may at first be no more than a sketch but soon becomes complicated by constraints, details and, not infrequently, enhanced expectations. What began as a straightforward family car can easily grow into a complex driving machine. For the teacher the design brief can usually be seen as the syllabus or curriculum. This is the brief the teacher

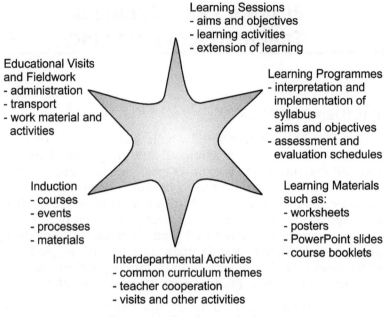

**Figure 14**: *Teacher as designer*

has to respond to. How many times have you heard a worried colleague say 'I don't know how I will finish the syllabus'. The implication here is that if the syllabus is not completed, the examination results will be prejudiced and who knows what else besides.

The only problem with this rather mechanistic approach is that it misses out what this book (and education as a whole) is all about – learners and learning. So let's talk about them.

## DESIGN FOR LEARNERS AND LEARNING

In addition to the requirements of the syllabus you are using, the learners themselves add to the design brief. Traditional didactic teaching methods took little account of learner needs. Work was handed down irrespective of the differing natures of the learners, their motivation, aspirations, interests, skills, learning styles or social background. Modern teaching-learning methods pay close attention to such needs as our success in meeting them can radically affect the quality and extent of learning. Of course we need to meet the requirements of the syllabus but that alone is pointless if our learners actually learnt very little in the process. Someone once said that *'Learning is not a stadium game'*. Yet we know that it is all too easy for teaching to subside into mere 'spoon feeding'.

So how do we accommodate both the needs of a syllabus and the needs of our learners? The answer has to be — through more effective design.

In the first place, effective design relies on a firm understanding of what you are trying to achieve. This involves a clear grasp of the syllabus, what its aims and objectives are, the knowledge, skills and understanding involved and the assessment objectives and methods. It should then be possible to relate syllabus topics to the timeline of your Learning Programme Plan. You will also need to get a clear early picture of your learners' skills, knowledge and understanding. You can achieve this by talking to their previous teachers, consulting assessment records, carrying out diagnostic tests, interviews with learners and so on. Out of all this you can design your Learning Sessions.

## DESIGNING LEARNING SESSIONS

There is no one way to go about this. Some teachers are very 'goal orientated' in their design thinking. They identify a set of Learning Outcomes and their Learning Sessions are engineered towards achieving these for their learners. These 'Outcomes' are in fact geared to Learning Objectives which are set out in the Lesson Plan and are stepping stones to securing the Aims of the Learning Session. Contrast this with another approach which at first considers the syllabus topic with the learners' needs and then imagines Learning Activities which generate Learning Outcomes. This is an attempt to 'visualise' activities rather as dramatists or film directors work.

Objective chaser or film director, the focus of your design should be the Learning Activities and it is for you as the teacher to set these up. This is where the creative bit really kicks in! The learners cannot just wander into the class and devise activities for themselves and the syllabus will not give you a design for every learning session. You therefore become a designer and then a manager of Active Learning.

All designers have to bear in mind Design Parameters. Many people will immediately see these as a series of constraints. In fact they do include constraints but there is more to it than that. The parameters define the outer edges of the design 'Box'. For example our Learning Activity might be engaging learners in studying a particular historical theme. We should take care not to stray too far beyond the theme in terms of content otherwise: (a) we might overload learners with material; (b) we might stray too much into the subject areas of future Learning Sessions, and; (c) we might prejudice management of learning time. Constraints will clearly involve consideration of time, resources, feedback, etc. Be realistic about these but don't see them in an overly negative way. The writers have seen Active Learning take place on a beach with nothing more in the way of resources than pencils, notebooks and some sharpened sticks to draw diagrams in the sand!

Your design for a Learning Session should therefore include:

- the Aims and Objectives of the Learning Session. Here 'Objectives' are phrased as 'What the learners will be able to do by the end of the lesson (to reach its Aims)'
- an introductory few minutes which show where the class fits into the overall Learning Programme, what the Learning Objectives are, what the learners will be doing and the Learning Outcomes to be reached
- an explanation of the learners' Learning Activities and how these are to be resourced and managed (especially in terms of time)
- how the lesson is to be summarised and important learning points to be reinforced – plus any extension of learning, say through homework.

## CHECKING YOUR LEARNING SESSION DESIGN

There are some Key Questions you should ask yourself about a simple Learning Session design. These are the kind of questions which Observers and Inspectors might ask you about.

- What are the learners actually doing? Are they clear about what they are supposed to be getting on with and what they are supposed to be producing? In many classes the learners do not seem to be directly involved in the learning session.
- How do we know that learning has taken place? What, if any, form of assessment is to be used during or after this Learning Session?
- Empathy? What would it be like to be a learner during this session? Can I get help and/or reassurance? Can I get extra materials? Can I get a reprise of the time schedule or objectives of the Activity?
- How flexible was the design? Could it deal with unexpected developments such as an interesting learner question which needed a lot of explanation, a difficulty with an audio-visual aid, a brief visit from someone else?
- What about feedback from your learners? How are you going to arrange this, record this and discuss this?

## A SAMPLE DESIGN OUTLINE

This outline was carried out for a class of 25 ten-year-olds (in which one of the writers was a learner!) The Activities outlined below were carried out in a sequence of learning sessions over a number of weeks. The school was very modern in its educational outlook (for the time). For the moment just think about the sequence of activities and what the learners might gain from them in terms of knowledge, understanding and skills.

(a) A study of two maps – one a regional map, the other a detailed map of a small area within that region. How to locate places using grids: Learners work in groups to identify places and features.

(b) The large sheets of the detailed maps have been cut into 30 mm squares. Learners work in pairs to answer questions

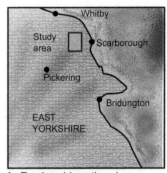

A. Regional locational map
showing study area

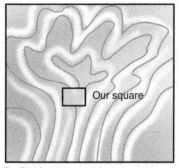

B. Study area ordnance survey
map showing 'our square' of
landscape

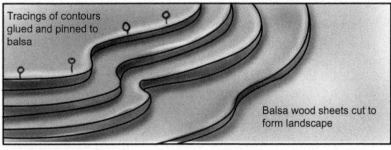

C. Construction of landscape square by cutting balsa wood sheets from
tracings of contours

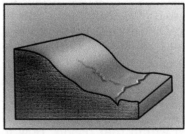

D. 'Stepped' landscape smoothed
by coating of papier-mâchè

E. Land use details added to
surface after field observation

**Figure 15**: *Construction of hardware model of
study area landscape*

about the contour pattern in their squares. They mark on tracing paper the 50, 100, 150, 200 foot, etc contours.

(c) Cut out with the scissors! Each pair cuts along the contours on the tracing paper and then pins the paper to sheets of balsa wood, taking care to ensure that further balsa layers can be piled on top to build a three dimensional model landscape. The layers can be glued together once all the cutting is complete.

(d) Papier-mâchè is applied to make the stepped balsa surface look more realistic. The area in question was on the southern slope of the North Yorkshire Moors.

(e) When dry, the papier mache surface was painted in a neutral colour. Excitement mounts as the learner pairs compare each other's squares.

(f) The big moment arrives when the three dimensional squares can be aligned into one giant model showing the topography and drainage of a large piece of countryside.

(g) The addition of fields, woods, etc to the squares comes when the class undertakes a three day field visit to the area to locate the squares, draw sketches of the landscape and take photographs which showed how the landforms had been formed.

(h) The whole model plus photographs, drawings and diaries formed the centrepiece of an exhibition at the annual parents' day.

There are a number of very important learning points for us as teacher-designers in the outline described above.

- This was a sequence of learning activities which was ambitious and original. It had a very simple origin – just looking at two scales of maps – but it unfolded into a more complex exercise and eventually into an exciting visit and a truly impressive final 'product'.

- The activities were straightforward and most kinds of learners could develop their skills. Notice the considerable range of kinaesthetic skills used here. Some educationalists believe that such skills may be preferred by over 50% of learners.

- As the model landscapes appeared in the classroom learners asked questions about the formation and features of their piece of landscape. These were further explored in the field visit.

- There was no formative assessment beyond teacher guidance and reassurance but diaries, drawings and a final project account were assessed and reported upon.
- Notice that the learners undertook (literally) a learning journey. This can be a very powerful learning experience.

ON REFLECTION

Look back to Figure 14 in this section. See if you can construct a MIND MAP of your own professional activities which involve an element of design. We will give you a start. Assessment will probably call on your design skills. Next think more broadly about your own professional activities beyond the classroom environment. Is there a design element in any of these and if so, what? Lastly, why not give some of your current Learning Session plans a health check and, if necessary, an overhaul in the light of what learners, observers or inspectors might discover?

## AIMS AND OBJECTIVES

We have already asked you to think about the concept of the teacher as a designer where the design brief, more often than not, is a syllabus. This means we need to be able to interpret a syllabus so the course and individual lessons can be planned. Syllabuses vary in content and can often be very detailed and complex but most express what the students must learn in terms of aims and objectives. However, it's not just a case of being able to interpret a syllabus. As teachers we may also be involved in its design and this means being able to write aims and objectives – not always an easy task.

AIMS

Many teachers find the distinction between an aim and an objective confusing. To help explain the difference let's take a practical approach using the diagram shown in Figure 16.

## Aim: Climb to the summit of Mount Achievement

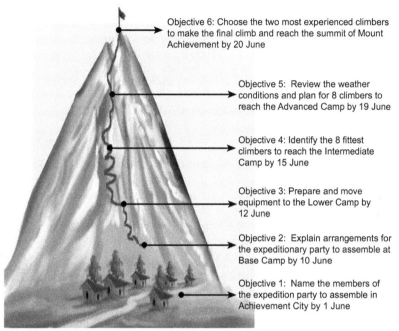

**Figure 16**: *Climb to the summit of Mount Achievement*

The aim *'Climb to the summit of Mount Achievement'* can be considered as a broad statement of intent. It tells us where we want to go, but not how to get there. For that we need objectives. We can see from the diagram that the objectives are very prescriptive and indicate what must be done to achieve the aim.

### Course aims

Most courses consist of a number of units, modules or subjects which are then broken down further into a range of topics. Before reaching all this detail in the syllabus most Awarding Bodies describe the overall purposes of the course by writing perhaps four, five or six course aims which are very general in nature. Reece and Walker (2003: p.196) describe a course aim as '...*a general statement which gives both shape and direction to the more detailed intentions of the course.*'

AN EXAMPLE – THE COURSE AIMS FOR A GCSE MATHEMATICS PROGRAMME

The scheme is designed to enable learners to:

- develop thinking, analytical and evaluative skills to solve problems in a range of contexts involving number, measures, shape and data
- use discussion to explain approaches, methods and answers to mathematical problems, identify difficulties and confirm understanding
- understand and use mathematical information
- calculate and manipulate mathematical information
- interpret results and communicate mathematical information

Whilst each of the course aims are related to the subject of mathematics and focus on the learner rather than the teacher, each one is written in such general terms it could cover several topics within the syllabus. It may be useful to remind ourselves of the course aims for the Cambridge International Certificate for Teachers and Trainers.

AIMS

The aim of the Certificate is to motivate and enable candidates to:

- develop as reflective practitioners
- update their professional skills through action and evaluation
- innovate in their professional thinking and practice
- share ideas and practice with colleagues

It is not unusual for a course aim to contain more than one verb but it should, and in this case hopefully does, give both shape and a sense of direction to the more detailed intentions of the course.

## Unit, module, subject and topic aims

As course aims are so general in nature each unit, module, subject or topic that go to make up the learning programme often have their own aims. Again they generally tend to be small in number but give more guidance to the teacher as to what the students are required to learn. Examples of unit, module, subject or topic learning aims could be:

The learner:

- appreciates how sound can add interest to a presentation
- knows current issues affecting the health and care sector

- understands how to use Windows software applications
- develops a range of skills and knowledge in beauty therapy techniques
- acquires a body of education theory that can be applied to professional practice.

If we were required to formulate some aims for a specific course such as a six unit teacher training programme it could look something like this:

The learner:

- appreciates how learning theory underpins professional practice
- plans programmes of learning
- uses a wide range of teaching and learning strategies to meet learners' needs
- understands and develops different methods of assessment
- develops resources and materials to support learning
- evaluates programmes of learning and their own professional practice.

You will note that it doesn't matter if it is a course, unit, module, subject or topic learning aim, it should always start with a verb. If you have to write your own aims for a learning programme you may find the following list of verbs, which is not exhaustive, quite useful.

TYPICAL ILLUSTRATIVE VERBS FOR WRITING LEARNING AIMS

| analyze | create | evaluate | perform | think |
|---|---|---|---|---|
| apply | demonstrate | interpret | promote | translate |
| appreciate | develop | know | provide | understand |
| comprehend | enable | listen | recognize | use |
| compute | equip | locate | speak | write |

We have seen that learning aims are very general in nature which makes them ambiguous and often difficult to interpret. They indicate a learning process rather than an outcome because the learning being described is not easily 'observed'.

## LEARNING OBJECTIVES

Learning objectives, which are also sometimes referred to as learning outcomes or competences, ideally describe observable learner performance and explain more precisely what the learner is able to do as a result of their learning. If you ask a learner if they understand Newton's three laws of motion they might say 'yes they do'. But what is it they understand? Can they simply recognize a definition for each of the three laws or can they explain in their own words how each law can be applied to a practical situation? The crucial point to remember when starting to formulate learning objectives is that ideally they describe the intended learning outcomes in terms of what the learners can do after a period of instruction. To explain what we mean, consider the following two examples.

---

EXAMPLE 1: AIM – UNDERSTAND NEWTON'S THREE LAWS OF MOTION

Learning objectives – the learner will be able to:
- recognise definitions for mass, force, velocity, momentum and acceleration
- identify the units of mass, force, velocity, momentum and acceleration
- solve practical problems involving mass, force, velocity, momentum and acceleration
- select Newton's three laws of motion from a list of definitions
- discuss Newton's three laws of motion using practical examples
- choose from a range of practical applications which of Newton's three laws of motion are applicable

---

EXAMPLE 2: AIM – APPRECIATE LEWIS CARROLL'S POEM 'JABBERWOCKY'

Learning objectives – the learner will be able to:
- read Lewis Carroll's poem 'Jabberwocky'
- express a personal opinion of the meaning of the poem
- relate the poem to the book *Through the Looking-Glass, and What Alice Found There*
- compare the meaning of the poem expressed by other writers
- discuss the context of the poem from the book in which it appears
- critically appraise an appreciation of the poem written by another writer

Both examples begin with an aim that indicates in a very general way what the students must learn. Each aim then has a number of learning objectives; each one being a mixture of student behaviour and subject content describing more precisely what the learners must be able to do to achieve the aim. Describing learning in terms of changes in student behaviour helps to make:

- what the learners do the focus of the lesson, rather than the teacher
- lesson planning easier
- the assessment of learning easier
- the evaluation of learning and teaching easier.

Some syllabuses, particularly those in the more vocational subjects, have the required learning written as **SMART** objectives where the acronym SMART stands for:

**S**pecific

**M**easurable

**A**chieveable

**R**ealistic

**T**ime-scaled

Some examples of SMART learning objectives are:

The student will be able to:

- write, in legible handwriting or by word-processing, with not more than five spelling mistakes, a 500 word essay on the theory of learning
- add and subtract two or more vulgar fractions and express the answer as a vulgar fraction in its lowest terms or as a mixed number
- prepare, cook and present for service a two-egg plain omelette
- fit correctly, within 10 minutes, a 5 amp plug to an electric kettle adhering to all safety procedures.

The following table summarises some of the advantages and limitations of using learning objectives to describe learning outcomes.

| LEARNING OBJECTIVES | |
| --- | --- |
| ADVANTAGES | LIMITATIONS |
| • provides a clear framework for the planning of lessons | • emphasises what students must learn, not how they learn |
| • unambiguous and can be shared with students to monitor and check learning | • can constrain the teacher in approaches taken to facilitate active learning |
| • useful for the acquisition and application of knowledge and skills | • not always considered suitable for describing higher level thinking skills |
| • informs the selection of teaching and learning strategies | • mechanistic approach may not help to achieve overall aims |
| • informs the assessment of learning | • detailed and time consuming to write |
| • provides clear standards | • may be given undue status |

We said earlier that syllabuses vary in the amount of detail they provide and the style in which they are written and it is not uncommon to read a syllabus where verbs such as know, understand, appreciate, etc. are used to illustrate learning objectives. This is because not all learning can be described in terms of observable behaviour, particularly in the higher level cognitive and affective domains of Bloom's Taxonomy.

## CLASSIFICATION OF LEARNING OBJECTIVES

We saw earlier in Section 1 how Bloom attempted to classify all learning into three domains: cognitive, psychomotor and affective. He then categorised each of the domains into different types of skills or abilities at different levels, from the highest to the lowest in what can be considered as a spectrum of task difficulty or 'ladder of learning'. Bloom's (1965) Taxonomy of Educational Objectives has had a tremendous influence on the way learning objectives have been formulated in syllabuses.

The following diagrams illustrate Bloom's Taxonomy in the three domains and typical verbs used to write learning

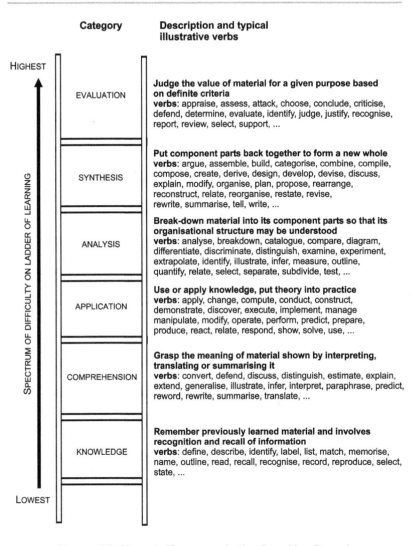

| Category | Description and typical illustrative verbs |
|---|---|

**Figure 17**: *Bloom's Taxonomy in the Cognitive Domain*

objectives in each category. It should be noted that some verbs can appear in more than one domain and in more than one category. This is because they are only illustrative of the domain and the specific level depends upon the context within which the verb appears.

The psychomotor domain includes some learning outcomes that are common to most subjects such as writing, speaking, etc. However, its major emphasis is in the practical craft subjects where the performance of a skill plays a prominent role. Typical verbs used to write learning objectives in each category of the psychomotor domain are shown in Figure 18.

Typical verbs used to write learning objectives in each category of the affective domain are shown in Figure 19.

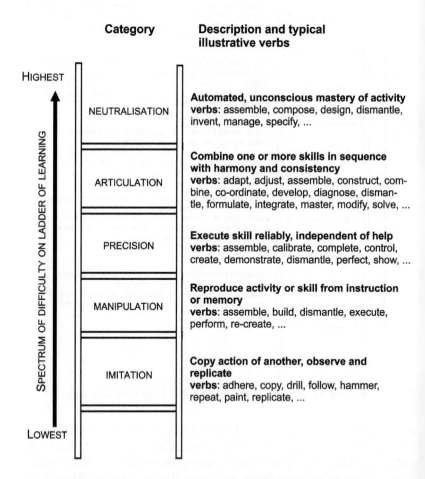

**Figure 18**: *Bloom's Taxonomy in the Psychomotor Domain*

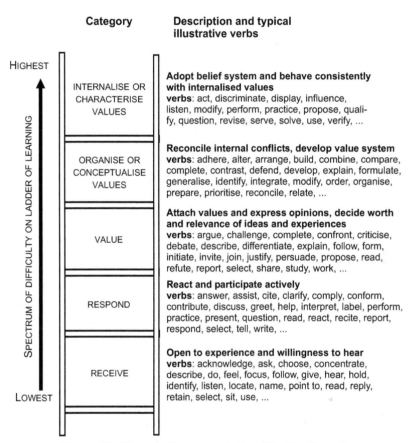

| Category | Description and typical illustrative verbs |
|---|---|

HIGHEST

SPECTRUM OF DIFFICULTY ON LADDER OF LEARNING

**INTERNALISE OR CHARACTERISE VALUES**

**Adopt belief system and behave consistently with internalised values**
verbs: act, discriminate, display, influence, listen, modify, perform, practice, propose, qualify, question, revise, serve, solve, use, verify, ...

**ORGANISE OR CONCEPTUALISE VALUES**

**Reconcile internal conflicts, develop value system**
verbs: adhere, alter, arrange, build, combine, compare, complete, contrast, defend, develop, explain, formulate, generalise, identify, integrate, modify, order, organise, prepare, prioritise, reconcile, relate, ...

**VALUE**

**Attach values and express opinions, decide worth and relevance of ideas and experiences**
verbs: argue, challenge, complete, confront, criticise, debate, describe, differentiate, explain, follow, form, initiate, invite, join, justify, persuade, propose, read, refute, report, select, share, study, work, ...

**RESPOND**

**React and participate actively**
verbs: answer, assist, cite, clarify, comply, conform, contribute, discuss, greet, help, interpret, label, perform, practice, present, question, read, react, recite, report, respond, select, tell, write, ...

**RECEIVE**

**Open to experience and willingness to hear**
verbs: acknowledge, ask, choose, concentrate, describe, do, feel, focus, follow, give, hear, hold, identify, listen, locate, name, point to, read, reply, retain, select, sit, use, ...

LOWEST

**Figure 19**: *Bloom's Taxonomy in the Affective Domain*

We mentioned at the beginning of this Section that there are occasions when we might be required to write learning aims and objectives when designing a course. Individual lesson plans can also be supplemented with learning objectives not in the syllabus but written by the teacher to add value to the students' learning experiences. This is where Bloom's Taxonomy of Educational Objectives can be really useful. As well as providing a basic sequential model for dealing with topics in the curriculum it also suggests a way of categorising levels of learning in terms of the expected ceiling for a given programme. Thus in the cognitive domain programmes of study at the lower levels may mainly cover knowledge, comprehension, application and some analysis, whilst on higher level programmes the emphasis will be on analysis, synthesis and evaluation.

However, there needs to be a note of caution here because sticking rigidly to learning objectives that do not go beyond the level of application, even on the lower level programmes, can be constraining. It is important, no matter what the level of programme students are studying, to include the full spectrum of knowledge, skills and attitudes through task design, as learning is not just about subject content. The classroom is a dynamic environment and whilst the students may be learning how to divide a line 20 centimetres long into ten equal parts, the teacher will also be helping them to develop other attributes such as using their creative and critical thinking skills. These skills are high on Bloom's taxonomy but are not always made obvious in the syllabus. Ideally subject content is taught so that it encompasses the development of a whole range of skills, knowledge and understanding which are all part of human development. Petty (2004: pp. 402) puts this into perspective when he emphasises that 'How you teach is more important than what you teach. It is what the students' do that decides what skills they learn, not the topic.' As useful as Bloom's taxonomy may be when writing learning aims and objectives it is important teachers do not become slaves to the system of classification, it is a guide not a master.

Hopefully after reading through this Section you will find the distinction between an aim and an objective less confusing. You may have noted in examples used earlier to demonstrate the difference between an aim and an objective, they spanned the whole spectrum of Bloom's taxonomy in the cognitive domain. As a reminder here they are again.

| EXAMPLE 1: AIM – UNDERSTAND NEWTON'S THREE LAWS OF MOTION | |
| --- | --- |
| **Learning objectives – learners will be able to:** | **Ability level** |
| • recognise definitions for mass, force, velocity, momentum and acceleration | knowledge |
| • identify the units of mass, force, velocity, momentum and acceleration | comprehension |

- solve practical problems involving mass, force, velocity, momentum and acceleration — application
- select Newton's three laws of motion from a list of definitions — analysis
- discuss Newton's three laws of motion using practical examples — synthesis
- choose from a range of practical applications which of Newton's three laws of motion are applicable — evaluation

| EXAMPLE 2: AIM – APPRECIATE LEWIS CARROLL'S POEM 'JABBERWOCKY' | |
| --- | --- |
| **Learning objectives – learners will be able to:** | **Ability level** |
| • read Lewis Carroll's poem 'Jabberwocky' | knowledge |
| • express a personal opinion of the meaning of the poem | comprehension |
| • relate the poem to the book *Through the Looking-Glass, and What Alice Found There* | application |
| • compare the meaning of the poem by other writers | analysis |
| • discuss the context of the poem from the book in which it appears | synthesis |
| • critically appraise an appreciation of the poem written by another writer | evaluation |

You could now go back to the original example and see how the objectives used to achieve the aim of climbing Mount Achievement also covered the full spectrum of Bloom's taxonomy in the cognitive domain. Just as the climb gets harder for the expedition party as they go up the mountain, learning also gets harder for students as they engage in activities that are designed to climb the ladder of learning.

Finally, try this short activity which requires you to recognise aims and objectives to check understanding and reinforce learning. The answers can be found in Appendix 2. If you identify 9 or more correctly, well done. If you still find the distinction between an aim and an objective confusing don't worry but perhaps discuss with a colleague or mentor the concepts before reading through this Section again.

**Activity**

Identify in the following table which are aims (A) and which are objectives (O) by circling the appropriate letter.

| | | | |
|---|---|---|---|
| 1. | Know the difference between an aim and an objective | A | O |
| 2. | Be able to translate a selection of French menus into English | A | O |
| 3. | Know how to prepare, cook and present for service a two-egg plain omelette | A | O |
| 4. | Understand the principles and methods of assessment | A | O |
| 5. | Be able to list, in order, the health and safety procedure for someone who has had an electric shock | A | O |
| 6. | Be able to draw a colour wheel using the four primary colours | A | O |
| 7. | Develop skills in writing business letters | A | O |
| 8. | Appreciate the problems of world pollution | A | O |
| 9. | Know how to place data from other files into the correct place in a document | A | O |
| 10. | Be able to write, in legible handwriting, a 1500 word essay on the theory of memory in learning | A | O |
| 11. | Know the operation of an internal combustion engine | A | O |
| 12. | Solve a quadratic equation using more than one method | A | O |

# THE CHANGING ROLES OF THE TEACHER

The impact of the modernisation of education and society has been to multiply and diversify the roles of the teacher such that many practitioners have come to see the profession as being very stressful. Most readers will recognise the multiplicity of demands made upon work time by the implications of Figure 19. Indeed you can amuse yourself by highlighting the areas which apply to your own working context and adding others which we as authors have omitted. This multiplication of roles prompted the designers of the Certificate qualification to design

Unit 3 which is entitled 'REFLECTING ON PRACTICE' and gives teachers a chance to look at their professional work beyond the classroom, for instance in inter-departmental co-operation or designing schemes of assessment. We will look at Unit 3 in sharper focus in Section 5.

One thing is certain about the implications of Figure 20. You can bet your bottom dollar that practitioners in any

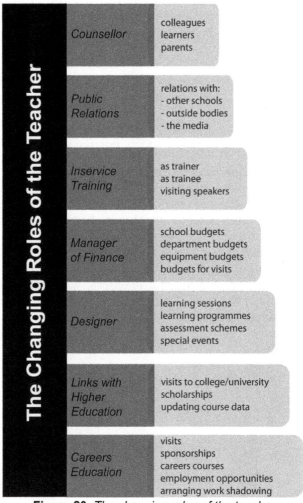

**Figure 20**: *The changing roles of the teacher*

other profession can bemoan something all too similar! In a sense this explosion of responsibilities is only to be expected. As economies and societies modernise they become more sophisticated throwing up new technologies, opportunities and expectations. These breed new professional activities. There are certain upshots of this situation which teachers need to know about and act upon.

- As we can see the teacher now has a growing number of roles which reach well beyond the classroom.
- Note that – most if not all – these roles can be seen as professional activities in which group (team) work is the norm.
- You may find yourself involved in all or some of these roles. Highlight these and add-in any other which you have collected!

## MANAGING YOUR LIFE AS AN INDIVIDUAL

The Greek philosophers urged us to 'know thyself'. This is obviously an excellent starting point in any self appraisal but it is difficult to develop the idea much further. Indeed you might think that this has no place in a book about the development of learning. But if you are going to dip into this book and say 'good ideas but I haven't got time to do anything about them' then we really have got a problem and it is shared by many thousands of other professional teachers, who will claim they have problems of 'work-life balance' or as it should properly be termed, 'work-life imbalance'.

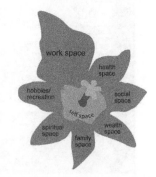

**Figure 21**: *Life-work balance*          **Figure 22**: *Life-work imbalance*

Take a look at Figures 21 and 22 which shows your life as a series of 'spaces'. Each 'space' represents an activity area which occurs to a greater or lesser extent in all our lives. The spaces are drawn as petals on a flower. Interestingly most successful people are able to give attention to many petals in their lives. As well as being a famous footballer, David Beckham promotes products, works for charities, has founded a soccer academy and is something of a family man, too. If the work petal in your life looks like the one in Figure 21 then you need to take some action to restore your work-life balance! Perhaps then you will have time to be refreshed and develop your potential to help develop learners and learning.

One response to the above might be immediately negative. Readers might say 'by asking us to develop our teaching-learning techniques, say by undertaking your Certificate, you are simply overloading our work petals even more!' Both authors of this book have been in this position and we have every sympathy with those in the midst of it. However, there are ways out of it, there are things you can do about it and you can be more effective as a professional teacher. We would ask you one question to take around with you after reading this section whatever your professional teaching context and it is this:

*'What other concern is more fundamental to your work as a professional teacher than developing the ways your learners learn?'*

We all have constraints upon our lives but we all have a 'self space' in the middle of our 'Life Flowers'. In this space we can reflect upon the emphasis we give to each petal and the energy we put into it. The flower's shape is driven from within us and it will respond and reshape if we are proactive. If we want to develop our professional practice we can and here are some ideas to help you.

## RECORDS AND REFLECTIONS

Buy an exercise book or a large pad and use it as a REFLECTIVE JOURNAL. When it runs out buy another! Keep it with you for instant reference. Use it to record what went well, feedback you got from learners, stuff you have learnt from colleagues, material you have googled, references from books and newspapers. Write about what you do – you will find it will give you a whole new dimension to your life as a professional. You will want to learn with your learners instead of superimposing material on them. But always write it down. This evaluative evidence is vital to the development of learning for your learners. Nothing else matters as much as this. Too often teachers have paid lip service to evaluation as an essential ingredient of development. It has been squeezed out of our work, perhaps so that we can give more time to 'finishing the syllabus'. Teachers often finish the syllabus but how many of their learners actually get there? And in what sort of shape? By 'drill' and 'force feeding' of material and ideas? How effective and rewarding are these methods for teachers and learners?

As we have said elsewhere in this book, many teachers still confuse evaluation with assessment. If ongoing evaluation was part of professional practice this confusion would never occur. It would be crystal clear that the latest formative assessment outcomes or project grades were merely evidence for evaluation of the learners' progress and the effectiveness of the learning programme. Reflection upon practice brings about evaluation. You can reflect in several ways:

- write short notes of ideas and outcomes after or even during lessons
- summarise ideas and inputs from colleagues or meetings as necessary
- write out points of evaluation at the end of learning modules or semesters
- large scale evaluation at the end of courses or learning programmes.

These reflections are usually individual – especially after learning sessions, though we all learn immensely by discussing the effectiveness of our practice with those who observe our work. Sharing reflection is vital at the end of learning programmes so that improvements can be set in train for the next sequence of sessions. In fact the more frequently you reflect the more Kolb experiential cycles you and your learners will go through and the quicker you will be able improve your practice and your learners' involvement. It's not unlike 'tweaking' (tuning) the engine of a competition road car!

## MANAGING YOUR OWN PROFESSIONAL TIME

It is simply no use attempting to change your own or your learner's practice if you cannot make the best use of their and your own time. It is no use saying 'I haven't got enough time.' You might have if you were better organised. Here are some steps you can take to be more effective as a professional teacher.

- Be better prepared. Take more time over design. Even having a fully worked session and programme plan is a massive time saving idea. People who know what they and their learners are doing can focus on developing their work as well as putting ideas into action. If rooms, resources and objectives are well prepared your learners can get into action from the first minutes and you can relax into support, assessment and evaluation modes.

- Be more focused at work. Avoid if you can 'office politics' and car park in-fighting. Try to work on assessment and evaluation while the evidence is 'hot'. Feedback to learners is far more effective if it is 'on the hoof' or immediately after formative assessment. This will help avoid the dreary business of taking marking home when you should be enjoying other petals in your Life Flower.

- Be able to prioritise tasks. Sort out your day and secure your main objectives. Be ready to say 'no' if you feel you will be of no use to an enterprise.

- Settle problems as soon as you can – especially learning and learner problems. Design ways forward and share concerns with colleagues and line managers if it is necessary.

- A smile is worth a thousand words. An enthusiast can be effective, even inspirational, if he or she works intelligently. Learners respond to warm-hearted people who help them to get things done by doing things properly themselves.

- Teaching itself and all the other new roles around it involve human interaction. This is invariably exhausting (as one of the authors found out at risk to his health). Do other things and get some sleep!

## MANAGING 'OTHER ROLE' TIME

- Where you have a choice of voluntary commitments beyond the classroom, it is better to concentrate on two or three and do them well rather than be over-committed and run into real problems of time management.
- Share activites with colleagues and develop team based tasks.
- Have clear time slots during the day/week/month which you will devote to other roles.
- Use design and evaluation skills and activities.
- Use and apply all the TIME MANAGEMENT advice listed above.
- Never promise what you know you will be unlikely to deliver!
- If you want to take on another role, be prepared to 'let go' of something else.

## POSSIBILITIES AND OPPORTUNITIES

Whereas it is possible to view Figure 20 as a series of pressures on teachers' time, it is also possible to see the 'changing roles' as a range of opportunities for teachers to develop their interests and professional skills. From Figure 20 we can draw up four areas of interest (and career development) which teachers might wish to specialise in beyond their work in the classroom. This may be a process of individual choice or institutional 'invitation' and note that there may be other areas in addition to the four we have listed and some teachers may prefer to spend their career only as class teachers – there is certainly nothing wrong with that.

Four Areas of Interest

- Managerial Role          – colleagues (eg subject department)
                                      – resources
                                      – activities

- Administrative Role    – academic and other records
  - – teaching timetable
  - – budgets and finance
- Counselling Role    – learners
  - – colleagues
  - – parents
- Public Relations Role    – school events
  - – school recruitment
  - – school liaison with 'outside' bodies

Each area presents fascinating opportunities for further career exploration and development but each would require a book of their own to do justice to their particular challenges and specialisms. However they do share certain characteristics which certainly are the concern of this book and of the Certificate for Teachers and Trainers.

- However indirect the links may seem, they are all there to benefit the development of learning and we must not lose sight of that central aim.

- Each area usually thrives when teachers work together. Teamwork can help speed the delivery of tasks and enhance the quality and sophistication of outcomes.

- As teacher roles multiply so does the need for specialist knowledge, skills and understanding. To meet these needs professional associations, conventions and qualifications have developed and practising teachers are urged to make use of them at local, regional or national level. The Internet has vastly helped their accessibility and effectiveness.

- Each area can be improved in practical terms by using the basic steps which we use in the teaching-learning cycle elsewhere in this book. Of course we may not be looking at learner assessment here but we most certainly will need to design, practice and evaluate.

- Each area will require even more judicious use of time which brings us back to thoughts of work-life balance and time management with which we began this section.

## USING GROUP WORK

There are many situations in which learners can carry out learning tasks and achieve learning objectives. This kind of teamwork also helps prepare learners for activities in many walks of life including social activities, charity work and the workplace. Nor is it limited to human beings! We know that many species hunt in teams. Hyenas and wolves live and hunt in packs and dolphins work together to drive shoals of fish towards the surface of the ocean. Many learners (including adults) really enjoy working together and this technique is frequently used in Active Learning. You can develop your own way of using groups but here are some ideas to start you thinking.

### GROUP SIZE

Clearly, the optimum size for learning groups will vary according to the learning task, age of learners, resource constraints and opportunities and the needs of the learners. On the other hand we can relate a few generic findings. Working in pairs is a very useful technique, for example in creative and practical work but it is not technically *group work* so we will move on. In general most teachers and trainers regard a group of three as being awkward. Usually two individuals form an alliance and one gets left out. In general FOUR seems to be a comfortable number for most people. As one teacher put it 'small enough for the bold to shine and big enough for the shy to hide'. It's an oversimplification but we can easily see what is meant, probably because we have all been there as learners. Usually this group size is easily resourced and managed. If tasks are more complex, it may be necessary to use teams of six or more. For example some design and role play tasks may need learners with mixed and more specialised skills and interests.

### GROUP ROLES

Many quick group work exercises often have no need for recognition or use of different individual roles within the group as a whole. All that most require is a spokesperson or collator of ideas/notes. However, once groups are used in more demanding or complex work then roles do become important and this might well affect the issue of GROUP MEMBERSHIP.

- Time manager
- Researcher
- Ideas generator
- Chairperson
- Task evaluator
- Production manager

These are six possible roles but there are more and some interesting research particularly by Meredith Belbin has been carried out on this fascinating topic.

Most practising teachers will wish to mix group members for more immediate considerations such as:

- gaining the most effective mix of learner personalities, aptitudes and abilities
- separating possible sources of abrasion or conflict
- enabling newcomers to mix more readily together
- enabling peer learning to take place.

## GROUP DYNAMICS

Many teachers and trainers will recognise the four stage model:

- **Forming** – the group gets together and individuals get to know each other.
- **Storming** – competing ideas are identified and discussed. This is often characterised as 'brainstorming' or 'thought showering'.
- **Norming** – the group agrees on common ground and accepts a pattern of work or ways forward.
- **Performing** – the action or production phase when agreed ideas/processes are actually used to achieve (learning) tasks.

As practising trainers, the writers would add that these four stages are not always evident in learning groups. Some teams can be harmonious from the outset and enjoy their time together, working easily towards their objectives. Don't count on it, however! It has to be said that some groups have difficulty in achieving all or even some of the four stages! You may well need all your professional diplomatic skills to negotiate a productive way forward in a group riven by differences of personality and approach. Even the most sophisticated knowledge of learner needs cannot obviate some of the interpersonal spats which can arise in this type of work.

Inter-group competition very often arises as a matter of course. As long as it is properly managed it can be used, say in peer assessment of group presentations. Friendly competition is no bad thing as long as it aids the achievement of learning outcomes. Group Leadership is, again, a very specialist issue. It has many connotations beyond education. In the writers' experience it is perhaps better to avoid use of the term 'leader' in everyday use of group work and use 'representative' or 'rapporteur' instead.

## MANAGING GROUP WORK

This is not easy. The very mention of 'group work' changes the working atmosphere in a classroom. Feet shuffle, looks are exchanged and immediately learners begin to wonder which group they will be in and with whom. It is as well to resolve the issue of group membership at the outset of the learning session so that learners can then focus on the activities themselves. If furniture has to be moved it should be at the very start of the learning session. Ground rules should be established as to the permitted level of noise.

### 1. Instruction

The most common cause of group misunderstandings is a failure to give clear objectives, clear operational instructions and a very clear time frame before the groups get to work. Leave instructions on a PowerPoint slide, whiteboard or flipchart so that everyone can remind themselves of what is required as the group exercise unfolds. This will also save the teacher and the learner time in not having to ask and answer simple questions.

In essence the learners should be familiar with:

- ➤ the learning objectives to be achieved
- ➤ any knowledge, skills or understanding necessary for developing their work
- ➤ availability of and access to resources
- ➤ the timeframe for the activity
- ➤ the learning steps to be used
- ➤ any formative assessment to be used
- ➤ how to access your help and guidance.

## 2. Facilitating group work

There are many ways of setting up group work in a learning environment. Here are two simple approaches for you try out in your own professional context.

➤ The direct method

This method involves learners joining their group and feeding in individual input in the form of ideas as the learning session unfolds. It means the group can get into action immediately and thus might be seen to be saving time but not everyone thinks usefully and productively 'from cold'. Sometimes it suits the task- for example in types of field measurement and surveys where time and swift decision making are of the essence. The same may be true of many forms of practical work in the laboratory or workshop.

➤ The step method

This approach involves *three* practical stages illustrated in the following diagram.

By pre-considering ideas the group can then really do what it is good at – assessing ideas, refining and clarifying notions and getting something done about them. There is a lot to be said for silent individual focus at the beginning of group work. It ensures that everyone has a contribution to make and people have time and space to think. (See also our section on bringing creativity into the classroom). It also helps to counter any aspect of rule by the most egregious or outspoken group members.

```
┌─────────────────────────────────────────────┐
│        Silent Individual Contemplation        │
│   of the task or problem assigned to the group │
└─────────────────────────────────────────────┘
                      │
                      ▼
┌─────────────────────────────────────────────┐
│            Sharing Ideas in Pairs             │
│   sorting-out and agreeing on favoured ideas   │
└─────────────────────────────────────────────┘
                      │
                      ▼
┌─────────────────────────────────────────────┐
│   Pairs Submit Favoured Ideas to the Group    │
│    and the group discusses the merits of these │
└─────────────────────────────────────────────┘
```

### 3. Time management

Most groups find the management of time very difficult. Group work requires multi-tasking from everyone and it is easy to lose track of time. It is often useful to remind groups of time elapsed and remaining time as you see fit. If guidance to all or some of the group is given, make sure this is economical enough to avoid jeopardising the whole time frame for the group.

Many learning session plans either allow too little time for group work to really flourish or overload groups with learning objectives.

It is worth making the point to all groups that learning to work to necessary or agreed time limits is a vital set of skills – not least in examinations.

### 4. Feedback

There is nothing more frustrating for learners than to be given little or no feedback on all their group deliberations so it is important to design into the group work some form of identifiable outcome or 'product'. This might be a presentation, a performance, a gallery of artwork, some sort of video or artefact. This enables learners to learn from what other learners have achieved. They need time to make some record of this – and so does the teacher. If the group work has been particularly stimulating then ideas can be followed up (extended) in other forms of learning activities such as written work, further research, exhibitions of work, etc. And this takes time. Time management and allocation therefore becomes a leading issue in the design of group learning as a component in the sequence of learning sessions which form the Learning Programme.

## TYPICAL GROUP TASKS

There are hundreds of possible contexts in which group work can be used but just to get your imagination fired up here are just a few:
- problem solving
- development of case studies
- brainstorming
- developing a component of role play
- providing learner feedback via a focus group
- design work
- peer assessment group
- analysis of findings
- data collection
- working up a case for a debate
- developing a course of action.

It does not matter which level, age, culture or subject your learners are from, you will find that (properly designed and managed) learners can get to higher order learning skills very quickly through group work, that they take 'ownership' of the group's work and thus can recall its process and product relatively easily.

## CREATIVITY IN THE CLASSROOM

As we said in our Introduction, this book is written FOR practitioners BY practitioners. Our need for theoretical input arises from what we want to do – the development of our practice. Nowhere is this better seen than in the area of learning loosely termed *'creativity'*. Teachers feel comfortable with instruction, analysis, synthesis but mention 'creativity' and many are suffused by a grey mist of uncertainty. And this is not surprising for many are not too sure about the exact nature of creativity and where imagination leaves off and creativity weighs in. Yet creativity is an asset many of us desire and desire our learners to possess and nurture. Let us take this section in a few easy steps.

MYTHS ABOUT CREATIVITY

Some people associate creativity with certain subject areas to the exclusion of others. Arts subjects such as Fine Art, Music, Literature and so on seem inextricably linked to creativity. Perhaps this is because we have tended to personalise creativity by constant reference to iconic creative individuals such as Mozart, Picasso and Shakespeare. Howard Gardner uses this approach in his fascinating book *Creating Minds*. This is effectively saying that subject areas such as Mathematics and Science have no room for creativity – clearly nonsense! And while we are at it let's clear up the myth that only certain individuals are creative. In fact all our learners are creative or can be creative. Teaching itself is a creative profession – who is it that dreams up the Active Learning sessions for the learners?

We now reckon that the brain itself is much more complex than the stereotypical 'left brain for analysis, right brain for creativity' tag. The whole analogy of brain and computer seems entirely inadequate. We are dealing with something awesome and wonderful but how many of the buttons on our cerebral keyboard are we really pushing?

Our drawings in Figure 23 show the relationships between IMAGINATION and CREATIVITY. Imagination seems to be a kind of picturing ability which we (and no other animals) possess. The phrase 'mind's eye' is a convenient way to think of it. Imagination sets in train creativity but only when we are motivated to do something about our 'thoughts' or 'imaginings'. From the learning point of view, this motivational link is crucial. One of the most influential writers in the field of creativity is psychologist Teresa Amabile. Professor Amabile reckons that intrinsic motivation is critical in creative activity. In other words, you will power up your creativity by using your imagination if something is of real interest and/or enjoyment to you. So where does this feature in the world of learning where so much motivation is obviously extrinsic?

## CULTIVATING CREATIVITY

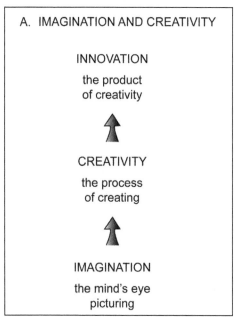

**Figure 23 A**: *Cultivating creativity*

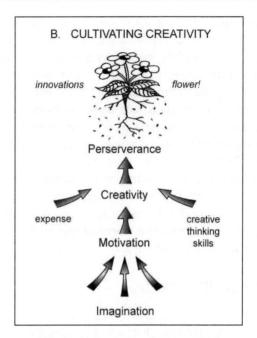

**Figure 23 B**: *Cultivating creativity*

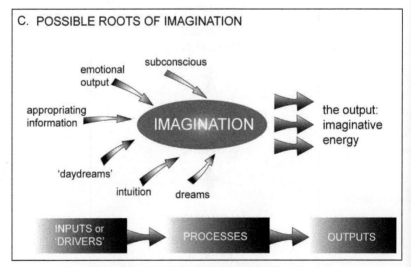

**Figure 23 C**: *Cultivating creativity*

## CREATIVE FRAMEWORKS

Experience has shown that simply telling learners to 'Use your own imagination' produces little or nothing in the way of creative response. It is a bit like saying 'here is a ream of paper, write a piece of fictional genius'. At least we've made some steps here – we've stated the medium and the outcome. We could 'scaffold' it further towards the learner and say 'Make your book like *War and Peace*'.

What we need here is a lot of empathy with and understanding of the learner. As teachers we need to stimulate creativity, specify outcomes and provide time, resource and support frameworks for our creative learners. We are getting right to the heart of Active Learning here. It is the learners who are going to be creative. We cannot be creative for them. We provide the crayons – we don't draw the pictures!

1. **Learner need**

   Clearly it is essential for teachers to ascertain and develop responses to the needs of individual learners but let us turn that idea inside out for a while. How many of us have asked 'What do you really enjoy doing?' and 'How do you like to do it?' Are we aware of the skills, interests and aptitudes which our learners possess or are we just looking at the assessment results of stuff we have given them? This seems an almost facile notion but are we really aware of what switches our learners on?

2. **Spelling out objectives and outcomes**

   Creative work is much like 'design' (See Section 2, page 46). There needs to be a 'brief', a specification of what the end product of a mass of creative processes is going to be. It could be a role play, a piece of music, an artefact, whatever. The stepping stones of how the learners might get there – some hints and suggestions might help provide developmental cues – a bit of 'scaffolding' if you like. You need to spell this out clearly so that the learners can relax into the tasks. Always remember to write out the objectives and outcomes somewhere handy so that the learners can refer to them during and after the session. You could use a PowerPoint slide (which you could print on request) or a worksheet.

### 3. Frameworks of time and resources

Whether you are writing a novel or designing a pair of shoes, most creative work needs a time frame and details of resource availability. Classroom work is no different and these considerations need emphasis in initial instructions to learners and judicious reinforcement during the learning sessions. Time is a very difficult dimension to manage for learners – they will need judicious reminders of how long remains for them to complete their work.

### 4. Stimulating creativity

Most people find it difficult to use their imagination and creativity 'from cold' – they need some friendly stimulation, some similar input to 'latch onto' (again, some scaffolding). You can try this out with your own learners and you might want to see how far these stimuli are linked to your knowledge of student learning styles.

Stimuli include:

➤ posters, paintings, photographs, drawings, slides
➤ artefacts including hardware model
➤ film, video, DVD
➤ written pieces including poems
➤ musical excerpts.

## EXTENSION OF CREATIVE ACTIVITIES

Creative work in class usually stimulates a great amount of emotional output on the part of the learners. There may be elation, wonder, admiration, disappointment and, more than likely, frustration. Learners often feel let down because they ran out of time or their group did not organise itself effectively. Many would like the experience to be extended so this is a vital consideration for your learning session DESIGN. Be aware that learners will feel let down if their work is not valued or seen to be in vain or simply wasted.

At a very simple level you can extend the activity through homework or after school use of the classroom facilities. Also you could develop it further down the sequence of learning sessions in your Learning Programme. At a higher, more demanding level, you could include the products of the creative sessions in exhibitions or demonstrations to larger in-school or public audiences.

Some ideas generated by the learners might be used to work up larger projects or assignments. In this sense the original learning session could be used as a pilot study for a whole raft of further work including more advanced and better targeted research. Extension involves sequencing and recharging learner-generated studies and can afford interesting and sophisticated opportunities for formative assessment and learner feedback.

## FACILITATING CREATIVE LEARNING

In an absorbing – and for us as teachers – vital article entitled *How to Kill Creativity*, Teresa Amabile defuses the myth that all you need to foster creativity is lots of resources and comfortable work spaces. She goes on to say:

> *'Indeed, a problem we have seen time and time again is managers paying attention to creating the 'right' physical space at the expense of more high-impact actions, such as matching people to the right assignments and granting freedom around work processes.'*

Professor Amabile is looking at a business environment here but her words have just as much significance for us as facilitators of creative activities in educational practice. Some big questions arise from the passage quoted above:

1. Have we designed our framework for creative activities clearly enough to match the right learners to the right tasks? Do we know our learners' aptitudes and interests well enough?
2. Have we got the right mix of skills and abilities in each group? Later in the same article Professor Amabile advocates a mixture of skills, aptitudes and interests in creative groups. As teachers we would add Learner Needs to this mixture.
3. What is the significance of the phrase 'freedom around work processes' for those of us in the classroom? Of course learners will need a physical atmosphere to let

their ideas flourish and the teacher's role would be supportive and encouraging. But then the bell sounds, the class ends and the creative bubble is burst. Maybe we need to let the mission rule the schedule more if we are really serious about including creativity in our educational aims. Professor David Hargreaves has written much about the school of the future which he claims may well be designed from the individual school level upwards and may include consideration of learning sessions very different from the usual 'class' or 'period'. This may help nurture creativity in the classroom. The Certificate offers chances to explore new ways of teaching and learning and creative work could well feature in these.

## ON REFLECTION

In the spirit of the Certificate, one of the authors was given the opportunity by the University of Cambridge International Examinations to design and contribute two workshops for senior and distinguished teachers at a large conference in Mumbai in 2008. Each workshop was to last 45 minutes and there were to be 25 delegates in each session. The theme of the conference was 'Learner Centred Learning' and the trainer chose 'Creativity in the Classroom' as his focus since it covered all levels of education, types of learner and subject area.

The structure of the workshop was very simple.

| | |
|---|---|
| **Step One** (15 mins.) | The relationship between imagination and creativity was explained using PowerPoint slides. |
| **Step Two** (15 mins.) | The delegates were divided into groups of four and using the STEP method of group work brainstormed ways in which creativity might be developed in class. |
| **Step Three** (15 mins.) | Each group then presented their ideas to the workshop as a whole. |

The response to the whole exercise was very positive and a variety of designs were explored. In fact such was the interest that some delegates deserted other sessions to take part and in the second workshop over 50 people wanted to attend causing searches for additional furniture and working groups in corridors!

One memorable piece of work came from a group who gave learners an opportunity to design, research, write, edit and produce a book on a particular study module. Certainly the workshops had ignited a great deal of interest, if not passion about using imagination and creativity but it proved a thought-provoking exercise for the trainer in that:

- not much provision had been made for the extra delegates in Workshop Two

- it was almost impossible to make a record of all the ideas the delegates came up with

- timing was a major problem as everyone wanted to have a say in Step Three

- there was no obvious EXTENSION of the workshops though who knows what was tried out in schools on the teachers' return from the conference and, to be very generous, it has at least been reincarnated in this book

- delegates seemed delighted to talk about teaching possi-bilities and had to be reminded that learners and learning were the focus of the workshop as well as the conference as a whole.

The whole workshop was a bit of a risk. It was very different from others on offer and the trainer had never used it before yet it was somehow inspirational and the trainer has been reading about creativity ever since! There's one other point to mention. Remember Professor Amabile's point about 'granting freedom around work processes'? CIE did not micro-manage the workshops. They were good facilitators and trusted the trainer to prepare and manage the sessions.

Reflections such as these are a vital component of the Certificate and the next time such a workshop is held the outcomes should be more complete!

## ASSESSMENT

Assessment is all about making judgements and it plays an important part in our lives. Even from an early age we are required to assess and make judgements on a fairly continuous basis, and generally we don't think twice about doing it. But if we did, would we always arrive at the same assessment decisions? And why is it other people don't always agree with our assessment decisions? If we asked each individual in a crowd of 10,000 people watching a football match to assess who they thought was the best player on the pitch they won't all agree with each other. Even more worrying is that every player on the pitch would more than likely be nominated by at least one person as the best player. So any assessment process is perhaps not as straightforward as we might always think it is.

As a starting point let's consider a definition by Ashcroft and Foreman-Peck (1994) who define assessment as

*'a judgement about the progress (formative assessment) or achievement (summative assessment) of a student's learning.'*

We could have used any one of a number of definitions of assessment produced by education researchers and writers but this one conveniently breaks down any judgement decisions into the two distinct phases of formative and summative assessment.

## FORMATIVE ASSESSMENT

Formative or on-going assessment is used to monitor and review the learning progress of students throughout the course and help future learning. It is useful to think of it as 'assessment for learning' and contrasts with summative assessment, which can be considered as 'assessment of learning'. The focus of formative assessment is on providing regular feedback to the learners about how well they are learning and what is needed to help and support future learning. It is also used to:

- reinforce learning
- motivate learners to learn and achieve
- provide regular feedback to the teacher on the effectiveness of the teaching and learning methods being used to help learners learn.

Providing learners with constructive formative assessment feedback, particularly the weaker learners, is an important part of the learning process. Having opportunities to praise the work of individual students and their learning, as well as identifying specific problems or weaknesses are key aspects of formative assessment which provide the basis for discussion between the teacher and the learner. Teachers need to allocate time to discuss performance and progress with learners as assessment without constructive feedback is of limited value. This communication is often of an informal nature in the class, workshop or workplace, but it can also take place effectively during scheduled one-to-one tutorial sessions, by letter, telephone or email. This is one of the great strengths of formative assessment because learners seldom receive any type of feedback from summative assessments, apart from the issuing of either a pass or fail grade. As far as the teacher is concerned, formative assessment can provide insights into what learning material may need covering again or identify the starting point for the next session.

We should not underestimate the importance of how formative assessment can be used in every lesson to help identify and plug 'gaps' in students' learning. Its importance is often reflected in the format of the lesson plan by having a column headed 'Assessment activity' to indicate the planned methods of assessments to be used at each stage of the lesson. An example is shown on page 88.

| TIME | TEACHER ACTIVITY/ CONTENT | LEARNER ACTIVITY | ASSESSMENT OF LEARNING | RESOURCES |
|------|---------------------------|------------------|------------------------|-----------|
| 0900 | Introduction – Share lesson outcomes | Directed questioning – recall learning from last lesson | Directed Q&A | PowerPoint presentation |
| 0905 | Introduce new topic – fractions | Discussion – practical experience of using fractions | Directed Q&A | Flipchart |
| 0915 | Facilitate activity | Game – identify parts of proper fractions | Observation and peer assessment | Flash cards |
| 0930 | Facilitate activity | Game – match fractions to decimals | Observation and peer assessment | Flash cards |

However, there is no point in being a slave to a lesson plan which requires the learners to develop new knowledge and skills if the existing knowledge and skills on which the new learning is built on is not fully understood. This is where students get 'lost' as they are unable to make the right 'learning connections'. Not fully understanding some fundamental 'threshold' concepts may have a major impact on all future learning. This is why many children can go through 10 or more years of schooling and leave compulsory education with poor literacy and numeracy skills. Race (2005: p. 26) calls this the 'ripple' effect because when a learner has 'gaps' in their knowledge and understanding, it often makes other subjects difficult to learn. This lack of understanding then spreads out to other subjects just like a ripple in a pond when a pebble is dropped into it.

## FORMATIVE ASSESSMENT METHODS

The most common and perhaps powerful formative assessment method a teacher has in their armoury is verbal questioning. When used effectively it is one of the quickest ways of checking and correcting learning. The problem is that too many teachers only pose questions that require the students to recall factual information and then give them insufficient time to think. They expect an answer immediately. This often results in the teacher rather than a student giving the answer.

It is also important to engage all the class in answering questions not just the dominant ones. Using assertive questioning where the teacher nominates who answers each question should ensure this happens. It is also a good idea, having received an answer from a student, not to confirm whether it is right or wrong but to thank them for the answer and then pose the same question to another student and ask them what they think. This ensures all the students have to think and can't 'switch off' as they may be called upon to answer. Effective questioning depends a great deal on the trust built between the teacher and the learners so that all opinions and views are acknowledged as valuable and worthwhile. Other points worth noting when using question and answer technique are:

- make the questions clear and concise using straightforward language
- give lots of praise when acknowledging an answer such as 'That's an interesting answer' or 'Good answer you are on the right lines' as it helps to motivate the learners
- use incorrect answers to pose further questions to correct misconceptions, don't automatically give the learners the correct answer or response
- involve shy learners by initially asking them questions they know the answer to and as their confidence builds pose questions where you think they may lack understanding
- start questions with 'why', 'how' or 'what' as they tend to be more thought provoking
- use both closed and open questions and try to construct them so they cover the full spectrum of Bloom's Taxonomy and as a result higher order thinking skills are assessed as well as knowledge and comprehension
- prepare a range of questions in advance when giving a demonstration or a lecture

- allow time for students to answer questions without immediately moving on to another student or answering the question yourself.

In most lessons teachers use a great deal of question and answer technique and direct observation as informal formative assessment methods to regularly check learning. The use of quizzes, crosswords, conferencing, matching games and self- and peer assessment also fall into this category. However, all informal methods need to be handled with care and sensitivity in operation because:

- learners are always wary of anything called a 'test' so informal methods are best embedded in learning sessions as part of an activity
- any assessment of the performance of a skill, particularly in front of peers, is very daunting for most learners
- using one-to-one techniques such as 'conferencing' can draw out emotional responses that can be difficult to manage and be very time consuming
- assessing group work is often difficult to manage and simple measures such as prepared tick lists are probably most effective and give the teacher an instant record.

The range of formal tests used for both formative and summative assessment includes:

- short answer questions
- long answer questions
- essays
- objective multi-choice questions
- oral questioning
- producing creative arts and artefacts
- assignments – problem-solving tasks
- observation of skills
- role play
- simulation
- portfolios including e-portfolios
- diaries and log books
- projects and reports
- computer-based assessments.

## FORMATIVE ASSESSMENT – ASSESSMENT FOR LEARNING

So why should teachers place so much emphasis on formative assessment? In 1998 a report titled *Inside the black box: Raising standards through classroom assessment* by Professors Paul Black and Dylan Wiliam of King's College London quoted evidence from around the world that formative assessment methods designed to improve learning (formative), rather than only measure it (summative), can raise standards. The report uses teachers' own findings to show how their roles as teachers, and the roles of their students as learners, have been transformed by new approaches towards assessment, particularly formative assessment. Four components of change recommended in the report that can improve learning can be briefly summarised as follows:

1. **Asking questions in class**

   Many teachers leave insufficient thinking time for learners to answer a question, often less than a couple of seconds, and frequently only elicit answers from a small minority. The research indicates that teachers who give students time to think about a question and devise strategies to ensure everyone participates not only allows students to apply their understanding in a wider sense but they, the students, think the teacher is more interested in what they think.

2. **Marking coursework and homework**

   Learners tend to focus on the grades or marks given by teachers and usually ignore any constructive feedback or suggestions for improvement. To improve learning teachers concentrated on only giving comments indicating how students were expected to take action to improve the work. This shifted attention away from competing for marks and merits and towards each using the opportunity to produce their best work. Some institutions now have a policy that no marks or grades are given on formative assessments.

3. **Students assessing one another**

   Peer assessment is a strategy many teachers now realise has a great deal of potential, particularly in group work, where students can identify and discuss common mistakes. Marking each other's work also allows the learners to think about what actual learning is required and what they need to do to meet the assessment criteria. The strategy of students assessing each other's work can be much more effective than waiting for a one-to-one tutorial with the teacher, which in reality may never happen.

### 4. Involving students in their tests

Most students dislike tests, formative or summative. However, involving them in setting test questions, inventing marking schemes and marking each other's work helps them to see tests in a more positive light. Whereas previously many students felt under pressure to succeed in a test they now use them as a way of checking their understanding of the work being covered confirming what they know and what needs further work.

The research by Black and Wiliam indicates that these four components of formative assessment add up to a powerful overall effect on transforming teaching and learning. Far too often in the classroom it is the teacher who is the most active and doing most of the thinking rather than the learners. Where the emphasis has shifted towards active learning and using formative assessment to support it, not only do the learners value the learning process more highly but they are also more likely to be motivated to learn. Other main findings of the report worth noting are:

- There are practicable ways to raise standards which do not involve 'teaching to the test' and embedding formative assessment within active learning enriches rather than narrows students' learning.
- Placing an emphasis on competition and competitive testing, which inevitably creates losers as well as winners, can damage learning. What's needed is emphasis on helping all learners to achieve their best. It is not enough just to set targets; learners must also be helped to reach them.
- Testing using conventional methods can help learning provided it is under the control of teachers so that they can align it with other ways of exploring students' learning needs.

## SUMMATIVE ASSESSMENT

Summative or final assessment is used to 'measure' students' learning at a given point in time and has the following characteristics. It is:

- usually taken at the end of a course, unit or module
- completed within a strict time frame
- carried out under strict supervision or invigilation
- undertaken with reference to all the objectives or outcomes of the course
- often only available to be completed once
- usually based only on formal methods of assessment
- assigned a grade or mark with no written feedback.

Increasingly summative assessment is becoming the main driving force behind teaching and learning. This is because learners tend to focus on passing their final exams and achieving a qualification and it is often what primarily motivates them to learn. For teachers the focus is now about getting their learners to pass summative assessments as they become increasingly more accountable for their learners' achievements. Clearly we do need systems of summative assessment that as far as possible determine or measure what the students have learned. But sadly this puts too much emphasis on the assessment of learning rather than assessment for learning and encourages teachers to teach towards final exams rather than the required learning objectives and outcomes. This often results in teachers regarding assessment as something separate from learning, and this is unfortunate. It can also cause a great deal of anxiety for learners, parents, teachers, education managers and employers because results can determine things like which school, university or job a learner can progress to, what future career prospects a teacher has, or how much money a school or college receives.

Summative assessment methods are the same as those used for formal formative assessment, but they are used for different purposes as indicated in the following table.

## COMPARING THE USES OF FORMATIVE AND SUMMATIVE ASSESSMENT

| USES OF FORMATIVE ASSESSMENT METHODS | USES OF SUMMATIVE ASSESSMENT METHODS |
|---|---|
| • provide feedback to teachers and students that required *learning* has taken place | • certificate or recognise *achievement* |
| • review/monitor student *learning* and take appropriate corrective action | • *certificate* 'safe to practice' |
| • improve the methods of teaching and *learning* to support learning | • *select* learners for progression |
| • reinforce *learning* | • *predict* future performance or selection |
| • motivate students to *learn* | • awarding of marks or *grades* |
| | • maintain *standards* |
| | • supply *quality* assurance data |

So how can we use summative assessments to help our teaching and support students' learning? Analysing past exam papers can be really useful when we are required to teach a new course because at the planning stage it provides us with guidance on the:

- level at which to pitch the learning
- types of learning activities that will promote active learning
- summative methods used to assess learning
- areas of learning that need frequent reinforcement
- timing for revision and when to practice exam techniques using 'mock' tests.

It is important not to place an emphasis on 'teaching for the exam' as this can stifle creativity and encourage didactic teaching and rote rather than deep learning. Having said that, we do have a responsibility to make sure our learners are properly prepared to take summative assessments at the appropriate times. A strategy we are all familiar with is to prepare 'mock' exam papers or skills tests that mirror the actual exams. In doing so, we can hopefully reassure our learners that the final exams should hold no fear for them. Unfortunately, if the formative assessment process is not rigorously monitored and reviewed students' learning mock exams can have the opposite effect and cause them unnecessary anxiety.

Increasingly, and often as part of a continuous assessment process, many teachers now have to devise and assess summative tests on behalf of an Examining Body. When devising formative assessments we rely a great deal on our experience to ensure they are 'fair'. But what do we mean by 'fair'? Devising summative assessments usually involves adhering to rigorous quality assurance procedures that tries to ensure tests are fair in terms of them being valid, reliable, sufficient and authentic.

## FAIRNESS OF ASSESSMENT

How many times have we heard our learners say after doing an assessment 'The test was not fair as some questions asked about things we hadn't been taught and in others we didn't understand what we were supposed to do'? To try and understand how assessments can be made fairer, because no assessment can be 100% fair, we will briefly consider the concepts of validity, reliability, sufficiency and authenticity.

### VALIDITY

Reece and Walker (2003: p. 321) describe validity as

> '... how well the test measures what it is supposed to measure'.

To put this into context a valid assessment:

- does not assess memory when it is supposed to be assessing problem-solving skills, and vice versa
- does not grade someone on the quality of their writing when writing skills are not relevant to the topic being assessed, but does when they are

*Ashok, I am aware your father is a stockbroker who says they only work in large round whole numbers but that does not make the test questions on vulgar fractions unfair nor is it an excuse for not doing them.*

- seeks to cover as many of the learning objectives and outcomes as practicable and does not rely on inference from a small and arbitrary sample
- has a weighted marking scheme related to the breadth and depth of learning being sampled
- has questions which learners can understand and are not culturally biased.

There is little point in conducting any kind of assessment unless we can be reasonably sure about what we are trying to measure. It is important that what we choose to assess is representative of what the learners have learnt and is linked to the learning aims and objectives. For example, if we were assessing the skills of a learner sending a text message, then using a written essay would not be an appropriate form of assessment. In this particular case a simulation, role play or similar activity is likely to be a more valid form of assessment.

## RELIABILITY

Reece and Walker (2003: p. 321) describe the reliability of a test as '... the extent to which it consistently measures what it is supposed to measure'. To put this into context, a reliable assessment:

- awards the same marks or grades to the same work when assessed by different examiners
- awards the same marks or grades to the same work when assessed by different examiners on a subsequent occasion
- sees the learners achieve the same marks or grades when the assessment is administered at different times.

If an assessment is administered to the same group twice in close succession we should expect some variation in the awarded marks or grades on the second occasion. This will be due to factors such as ill health, stress, inattention or similar reasons. Nevertheless, the same general trend in the pattern of assessment scores should be detectable if the assessment is reliable. When there is a long time-gap between assessments there is often a marked variation in an individual learner's score. Teachers normally establish pragmatically the reliability of the assessment measures they use. They may, for example, look at assessment grades, note a shift in rank order amongst their learners and then concern themselves with determining the reasons for any changes. In practice achieving 100% reliability is impossible, even using multi-choice objective tests. To increase the reliability of assessments a marking scheme with clear grading criteria needs to be produced and where possible shared with learners.

*I can't understand how I only achieved a test result of only 60% when I copied my sister Sonia's answers and she got 95%, life is just not fair!*

## SUFFICIENCY

It is difficult to design a summative assessment that tests all the learning objectives and outcomes from a whole year's work. Even when learners take two or more exams in the same subject it quite often comes to a point where we are guessing what topic areas will be assessed this time around. Some assessment methods such as multi-choice objective tests and short answer questions do lend themselves to a fairly wide spread of the syllabus, but long answer and essay questions do not. If required to design summative assessments, then to ensure sufficient coverage of the learning objectives at the appropriate levels we can:

- use continuous assessment that test 'chunks' of learning on a frequent basis – this does tend to make the learning programme very assessment driven
- use a combination of assessment methods such as multi-choice objective tests together with long answer questions –

care needs to be taken over issues of validity and reliability and if using a multi-choice objective test it should consist of at least 40 questions.

When designing formative and summative assessments the practical problems associated with implementing them also need to be carefully thought through. Questions like the following must be considered:

- Is the test easily administered?
- Is the test cost effective to produce and mark?
- Is the test easily scored or marked against well-understood criteria?

These practicalities usually present fewer problems with formative assessment. However, in the case of summative assessment the costs of producing certain tests may be high.

## AUTHENTICITY

A summative assessment taken under strict control exam conditions usually poses few problems when trying to ensure the work being assessed has been produced by each individual learner and is authentic. However, learners are increasingly being asked to submit work completed outside the classroom as evidence for all or part of a summative assessment. Judging the authenticity of this work can be difficult, particularly when a learner submits work that is significantly above the standard consistently produced in formative assessments. This is where an interview combined with using closed and open questions can help us to arrive at a fair assessment decision.

This technique can also be used for judging work carried out by a learner for formative assessment. The issue of whether a learner has copied the work of a colleague is often irrelevant. What's important is whether they have learned what you wanted them to learn? If you regularly mark and return formative assessments with supportive feedback you quickly get to 'know' a student and it allows you into their secret world. It is a privileged place to be and as Philip Beadle (2005) writes

*'Marking is the secret and special relationship between teacher and student. It is not in the public realm. You can't accidentally humiliate a child by privately praising what they have written.'*

Assessing group work is another area of assessment that can be difficult, particularly when making judgements on the contribution of each individual. Decisions about how to structure the assessment of group work needs to determine:

- What is to be assessed – is it the product, the process, or both, and if both what proportion of the marks are to be awarded for each part?
- What assessment criteria will be used and who determines it – the teacher, the learners, or both?
- Who will apply the assessment criteria and determine the marks – the teacher, the learners, or both?
- How will the marks or grades be distributed – a shared group mark, group average mark, an individual mark, a combination of two or more marks.

What is important is that all the learners are aware of the assessment methods and criteria being used before the group work activities begin.

Completing the table on p. 101 may prove useful when analysing assessment methods and help to reinforce the concepts of validity, reliability, sufficiency and authenticity. Any judgement made may change depending on the context, so use whatever you feel is appropriate for the subject you teach.

This type of activity can be used as part of the evaluation process required for each Unit in the Certificate for Teachers and Trainers programme. Asking teaching colleagues and learners (if mature) to complete the activity will potentially give valuable feedback data on which to base evaluative judgments. What's even more important is the potential impact this might have on future professional practice. Will you now use case studies, role play and peer assessment rather than traditional essay and

Key: **H** = high and **L** = Low

| ASSESSMENT METHOD | VALIDITY | RELIABILITY | SUFFICIENCY | AUTHENTICITY |
|---|---|---|---|---|
| Essay | | | | |
| Short answer | | | | |
| Objective multiple choice | | | | |
| Alternate choice | | | | |
| Game - matching block | | | | |
| Group project | | | | |
| Assignment | | | | |
| Practical skills test | | | | |
| Direct observation | | | | |
| Oral questioning | | | | |
| Case study | | | | |
| Interview | | | | |
| Role play | | | | |
| Quiz | | | | |
| Group presentation | | | | |
| Diary/ Journal | | | | |
| Audio/Video | | | | |
| Evidence portfolio | | | | |
| Self-assessment | | | | |
| Peer assessment | | | | |

short answer type questions as part of your future assessment strategy? Any analysis of fairness within an assessment process also needs to consider the differences between norm-referenced and criterion-referenced assessment.

## NORM-REFERENCED ASSESSMENT

Norm-referenced assessment compares one learner's performance with that of everyone else being assessed, and then places all the learners in rank order. Many public examinations where large numbers of candidates take summative assessments are still norm-referenced. This means the percentage of candidates being allowed to pass each year, regardless of the marks being achieved, remains the same.

Figure 24 shows what's called a normal distribution curve and ideally mirrors the spread of marks achieved by the candidates in an exam. In this example it has been decided that 70% of candidates achieving the highest marks will pass, 20% with merits and 10% with distinctions. The 30% recording the lowest marks will fail the exam. For norm-referenced assessments to

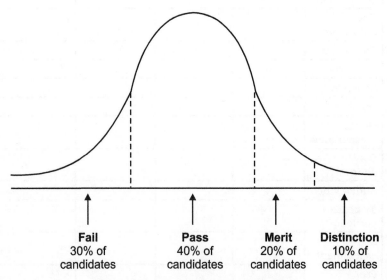

| **Fail** | **Pass** | **Merit** | **Distinction** |
| 30% of | 40% of | 20% of | 10% of |
| candidates | candidates | candidates | candidates |

**Figure 24**: *Normal distribution curve*

be as fair as possible there must be a good spread of marks and the questions must discriminate well between learners. If all the learners get marks above 70% or below 30%, then the system breaks down because it cannot then be used effectively to rank-order performance.

Using this system means the percentage number of candidates who pass the exam each year will remain the same, regardless of the marks being achieved. This has the advantage that variations in the difficulty of exams from year to year do not affect the grades or the numbers who pass. What can make it unfair is when there are lots of strong candidates in one particular year and a mark achieving a fail grade in that year may have recorded a pass grade in another year when the cohort of candidates was weaker. Another major criticism of norm-referenced assessments is that while it may demonstrate a candidate's relative standing within a group it says little, if anything, about what they can actually do.

As well as public examinations norm-referencing is used in situations where only a fixed percentage of candidates are allowed to 'pass' such as in the selection process for a job interview or the number of places available each year on a university course. This is where assessment decisions determining success or failure can have a major impact on a person's life.

## CRITERION-REFERENCED ASSESSMENT

In a criterion-referenced assessment if a learner can do what needs to be done to the required level or standard then they pass, regardless of how many other learners can or cannot achieve. So instead of doing any type of comparison a learner's work is assessed against specified criteria, which are independent free-standing definitions of what needs to be achieved. In theory all the learners could pass the assessment or they could all fail. As long as the assessment criteria are valid and reliable then criterion-referenced assessments are considered fairer than norm-referenced.

In order to have a better chance of succeeding learners need to know what is expected of them and what they need to do. Sharing the assessment criteria with them, or better still in formative assessments getting them to help formulate the criteria, can help to achieve this. If learners do not succeed they need to know which criteria they have not met. Although in recent years it has been common practice to make learners aware of the assessment criteria, many marking schemes still remain 'secret' to the learner, especially, though not exclusively, in public examinations.

As expected, criterion-referenced assessment has its critics. One of the major criticisms is that often the written criteria are unclear or ambiguous. Assessment criteria is  not easy to write, particularly where aesthetic judgement by the teacher is required. Despite the use of written criteria, assessment often remains a subjective activity. Critics also argue that those who design assessment tasks often fail to agree on the wording of the criteria and those who mark the work or performance often interpret the criteria in different ways. This is where a rigorous quality assurance system needs to be in place and samples of assessed work are re-marked or moderated by other teachers in an attempt to make the assessment decisions as fair as possible.

Most vocational qualifications now use criterion-referenced assessment supplied in the form of a rubric by the Examining Body. Many teachers are now devising their own formative assessment rubrics, which should be shared with learners, so they are fully aware of what is expected from them and what criteria their work will be assessed against. Using peer and self-assessment also allows us to involve the learners in the assessment process and this can lead to them assisting in the rubric design process. According to Pickette and Dodge (2009) one of the advantages of using this approach is that it '...blurs the lines between teaching, learning, and assessment.'

## COMPETENCE BASED ASSESSMENT

In vocational adult learning there is now an increasing emphasis on the assessment of competence. The analogy of the practical driving test is often used to illustrate a competence-based approach. In the UK, as long as a person is 17 years old and has passed the driving theory test, then there are few restrictions in taking the driving test. It can be taken at any time when the person feels ready to take the test. It doesn't matter who the teacher is, it could be a friend, relative or specialist trainer. The test can be taken without any specific training actually taking place if the person feels competent and is ready to be assessed. If they do not pass the test a person can keep trying until they do. Nobody is competing with anyone else. The driving test examiner is not concerned about how, when, where and for how long the person has prepared for the test. The examiner is only interested in assessing competence.

In a competence-based system assessment is independent of the mode of learning and the assessor or examiner uses national standards to assess performance. So competence-based assessment models look at what a candidate can do. The assessment needs to be under conditions as closely related to working conditions as possible, ideally in the workplace itself. Candidates are either competent or 'not yet competent' in relation to specific learning outcomes. While there are considerable advantages to a competence-based approach to assessment, there are also many concerns. One of the most contentious is the debate about degrees of competence. Some

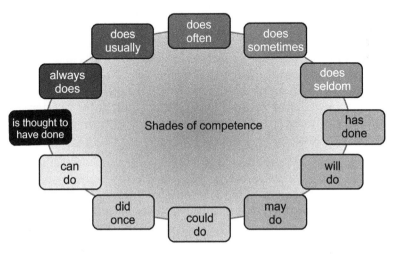

**Figures 25**: *Shades of competence (Race, 1993: p. 42)*

would argue that simply 'can do' is not enough and in this model there is no incentive to strive for excellence. Consider people in occupations such as plumbing, hairdressing, electricians, nursing or car mechanics, and the expectations we have of their competence. If somebody needs to call out a plumber in an emergency they understandably want a very good plumber, not one who once demonstrated competence according to what might be considered as minimum standards. In identifying what he calls 'shades of competence', Race (1993) highlights the difficulties in deciding exactly what we mean by competence as illustrated in Figure 25.

## PLANNING A SCHEME OF ASSESSMENT

We use a scheme of work to plan a series of lessons to achieve the course aims in the most effective way. In doing so we are attempting to provide our learners with a wide variety of learning activities to meet their needs. The same approach can be used when planning a scheme of assessment. Since many teachers do not associate assessment with learning they do not systematically plan for it, either when designing a scheme of work or for individual lessons using a lesson plan. We may see in a scheme of work how a teacher has planned for 'revision' to take place before a final (summative) exam by getting the students to do some practice tests, but this is not regarded as 'systematic' planning. Nor is the setting of the occasional homework (formative) indicated on individual lesson plans. Ideally all planning documentation should indicate what formative assessment methods are planned to be used and when. A scheme of assessment can be built into a scheme of work but it is becoming more common for it to be produced as a separate document.

One of the experiences that could be chosen as the activity for Unit 3 is to plan a scheme of assessment, either a sequence of formative assessments or a single summative assessment. What's important when doing this activity is that it gives you an opportunity to 'experiment', 'take risks' and through analytical evaluation, improve your and others' future practice. It could be you are teaching a lower ability group and have mainly used traditional assessment methods based on the learners answering long and short questions. Whilst this may test relevant knowledge, comprehension and application skills, it may also heavily rely on the learners' memory skills to be able to answer the questions. But having a good memory is seldom part of any assessment criteria, so why penalise students who can't remember a fact or mathematical formula to answer a question? Here is an opportunity for you to demonstrate how valid and reliable assessment questions can be constructed so as not to disadvantage such students. Students who have difficulty in expressing themselves in writing are also often at a disadvantage. This is where methods such as objective (multi-choice), oral and computer-based tests can be developed that assess the student's required learning and not their writing skills.

We have already suggested ways in which you could collect, analyse and evaluate assessment data. Remember you do not have to use the same form of formative assessment throughout a learning programme to achieve comparability or look at trends in individual progress. It is necessary to vary your choice of techniques as your assessment objectives will vary in type and emphasis. In doing so you could look at differences between observed and expected outcomes for various tests or measures. The amount by which the observed level of performance exceeds the expected level is known as 'value added'. Many see it as a reflection of effective teaching and it is a phrase which has had some currency recently. If you can design a sequence of effective, valid and reliable formative assessments for your learning programme, then the results of these will constitute some very valuable and powerful evidence for evaluation in the short and long term. The question you must ask yourself as a practitioner is 'How best can I achieve a series of ongoing measures which indicate the progress of my learners?' If you can research, design, operate and analyse your own custom-cut formative assessment scheme for a given learning programme then you will have proved yourself to be an effective facilitator and evaluator of learning activities – a very real achievement.

The emphasis in this chapter has been on formative assessment because it plays such an important part in the learning process. However, we have tried to stress that learning should not be assessment driven with teachers just teaching towards exams. This is because it stifles creativity and promotes an acquisition model of learning based on didactic approaches to teaching. This in turn means many learners have 'gaps' in their learning and the lack of structured assessment within learning programnmes often fails to pick this up until it is too late to do anything about it. But this doesn't mean we should just continually assess our learners and then do nothing to 'plug' the gaps in their learning. There is an old saying 'You don't make chickens fatter by continually weighing them.' No matter what type of summative methods are used at the end of a course for the assessment of learning we need to be more innovative and imaginative when designing our own methods of assessment for learning.

Hopefully you now have opportunities to refresh the whole idea of assessment by reflecting upon your innovative and well-considered practice because you:

- appreciate that assessment with a purpose is worthwhile
- value information accrued from assessment processes to improve future practice
- value the principles of well-designed and operated assessment techniques that make them as far as possible valid, reliable, sufficient and authentic
- realise the importance of feedback and how critical it is to communicate sensitively and succinctly with learners before and after assessment.

## FEEDBACK – SOURCES AND METHODS USED FOR EVALUATION

To evaluate teaching, learning or any other particular aspect of a course we need to gather evidence or data, both quantitative and qualitative. This information or feedback then needs to be analysed before recommendations for making any improvements can be made. The common sources and methods of feedback we use include:

- lesson observation – of teaching and learning by mentor, colleague, manager, teacher trainer
- learners – using formal and informal methods such as questionnaires and interviews
- assessment outcomes – results of students' formative and summative assessments
- keeping and maintaining a reflective journal.

## OBSERVATION OF TEACHING AND LEARNING

Observation of a lesson by a mentor, peer, manager or teacher trainer is the method usually used to gather feedback when evaluating teaching and learning. The observer usually works to some given criteria or checklist and the evidence or data collected is qualitative as it is subjective. The most useful lesson observations focus not just on the teaching but also on the learning taking place. The record of any observation can then be used as the basis for a professional dialogue between the teacher and the observer as part of the reflective process to learn and improve future professional practice.

The feedback from lesson observations, unless obtained from a well qualified and trained professional observer, do tend to focus more on the teacher's teaching skills rather than the students' learning. The teacher being observed, no matter how experienced, is also more likely to be interested in 'how did I perform' rather than 'did the students learn anything and were the learning objectives and outcomes achieved'. It is also a more straightforward task for an observer to provide feedback on the teaching skills being demonstrated than it is on the learning taking place. This is why so many lesson observation forms used to provide feedback on which to base a professional discussion or use for reflective practice are based on a checklist of questions or prompts.

A typical Observation Form is illustrated below where the observer notes comments under each heading:

| LESSON OBSERVATION FORM | | | |
|---|---|---|---|
| Name of teacher | | FT/PT | |
| Class | | Date | |
| Course/Programme | | Room | |
| Subject | | Time | |
| Type of class | | Class size | |

**1. Planning and preparing the session**

Evidence, strengths and areas for development

**2. Opening the session**

Evidence, strengths and areas for development

**3. Teaching and learning methods**

Evidence, strengths and areas for development

**4. Presenting material**

Evidence, strengths and areas for development

**5. Supporting students**

Evidence, strengths and areas for development

**6. Using activities and exercises**

Evidence, strengths and areas for development

**7. Using resources**

Evidence, strengths and areas for development

| 8. Relating to students |
| --- |
| Evidence, strengths and areas for development |
| **9. Promoting active learning** |
| Evidence, strengths and areas for development |
| **10. Managing the session** |
| Evidence, strengths and areas for development |
| **11. Assessing learning** |
| Evidence, strengths and areas for development |
| **12. Concluding the session** |
| Evidence, strengths and areas for development |
| **13. Evaluating the session** |
| Evidence, strengths and areas for development |

If an observation is carried out by an inexperienced observer they might want some help in the type of things to look for under each of the main headings and these can be found in Appendix 3. It is important to recognise that if using the checklist in Appendix 3 the list of questions under each heading is not exhaustive and could be added to or condensed. What is evident is that the range of knowledge and skills a teacher needs to plan and deliver a successful lesson is substantial. However, even if the answer to all the checklist questions is 'yes', do we really know that all the students have learnt what they are supposed to have learnt as the focus of each question is predominantly on the teacher and not the learning?

The checklist shown in Appendix 4 does put the focus of the observation on the learners and their learning. It could be used in conjunction with the checklist shown in Appendix 3 so any subsequent feedback does focus on both learning and teaching.

The checklists illustrated in Appendices 3 and 4 are very comprehensive so for Units 1 and 2 in the Certificate programme a more experienced observer might find the following checklist, used in conjunction with the CIE Observation Record Form, more user-friendly.

| OBSERVATION OF TEACHING AND LEARNING CHECKLIST | Y/N |
|---|---|
| • clear lesson objectives/outcomes shared with students | |
| • enthusiastic and interesting teaching which provides an enjoyable experience for the students | |
| • learning activities are suitable for all students, whatever age, ability or experience and are suitably demanding | |
| • teacher is aware of different individuals' needs | |
| • effective open questioning used to check students' understanding | |
| • all students are engaged and participate in the learning process | |
| • students demonstrate their achievements through improved knowledge, understanding and skills | |
| • skilful management of the classroom activities including discussions that ensure students' contributions are encouraged and valued | |
| • clear explanations, particularly of links between theoretical knowledge and its practical applications | |
| • teacher has up-to-date technical knowledge and skills | |
| • sensitivity to equal opportunities issues | |
| • clear writing on whiteboards/overheads, interesting and relevant use of Information Computer Technology including PowerPoint demonstrations | |
| • good quality handouts that are well produced, free from errors and contain references where appropriate | |
| • sufficient coverage of ground in the topic | |
| • effective management of any transition between individual and group work | |
| • crisp end to the lesson, summarising what has been learned | |

It must be recognised that when someone goes into a classroom to observe a lesson their very presence changes the dynamics of the situation. Teachers and learners often feel they have to 'put on a performance' and attempt to provide what they think the observer expects, and this will vary according to who that person is, such as a manager or teacher trainer. The use of team teaching as a method of observing learning and teaching can overcome some of these problems. This strategy encourages a professional dialogue to take place in a non-threatening way and is dynamic in its approach because any aspect of the learning programme, including future planned teaching and learning strategies, can be changed or modified at any time to suit the needs of the learners. Some teachers arrange for observed lessons to be videoed which can then be used to illustrate points in the feedback session with the observer. Alternatively it can be viewed privately when self-reflecting alongside making notes in a Reflective Journal.

The Certificate for Teachers and Trainers programme requires a qualitative CIE Observation Record form to be completed for each activity in each Unit by a colleague acting as a professional observer. This puts observation and the feedback used for subsequent analysis and reflection at the heart of the evaluation and learning process. It is important the professional observer is aware that the focus of the feedback is on the 'new' activity being tried out and the impact it has made on students' learning as well as the teacher's professional practice. They need to clearly identify what went well and what didn't, and explain why. It is also useful if the feedback indicates what the teacher might try to do differently next time to improve the facilitation of effective learning. This is why it is crucial to have an experienced professional observer who acts as a 'critical friend' and knows how to manage lesson observation feedback effectively as it can often raise sensitive issues.

## LEARNER FEEDBACK

Perhaps the most relevant source of feedback most often overlooked in any evaluation process is from the learners themselves. Most learner feedback made available to teachers in schools and colleges is obtained by students completing a questionnaire at the end of a learning programme. While this may yield useful information to inform future practice, it does not give the kind of immediate and dynamic information we often require to help improve teaching, learning and the course in general. Learner feedback also helps us to evaluate any learning session from three different perspectives. Petty (2004: pp. 242–43) calls this approach 'spectacles', as it looks at the same thing from different points of view. The concept is illustrated in Figure 26 below.

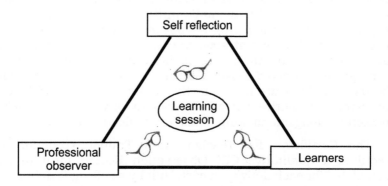

**Figure 26**: *Petty's 'spectacles' approach*

If using a questionnaire to be completed by the learners, it should be designed to give feedback on the teaching and learning methods used and involvement in the lesson. This means the emphasis is not on the personality of the teacher or their teaching skills but focuses on active learning and learner engagement. This does not preclude learners from commenting on the teacher's teaching skills but it is important to gauge how this has made an impact on their learning.

Questions need to be carefully formulated so that responses will be useful for the purposes of evaluation. For example, the question *'Did you enjoy today's lesson?'* may elicit responses such as *'yes'*, *'no'* or *'it was alright'*, but they aren't always that helpful. On the other hand, questions such as *'Indicate which one of the following activities you found most useful in today's session and briefly explain why: teacher demonstration, role play, small group discussion?'* are more likely to provide the sort of information that will be helpful in future planning. You can also ask open ended questions like *'What helped you to learn best in today's session?'* and *'What do you think needs to improve to help you learn better?'*

Consider the following example of a learner questionnaire or checklist used by a teacher to obtain learner feedback from a lesson where s/he is using role play for the first time combined with other activities.

---

LEARNER QUESTIONNAIRE

Please answer each of the statements with a 'yes' or a 'no'.

1. The introduction to today's lesson told me clearly what it was going to be about.
   **yes/no**
2. I knew throughout the lesson what I had to do.
   **yes/no**
3. The start of the lesson was interesting and gained my attention.
   **yes/no**
4. I enjoyed taking part in the role play activity.
   **yes/no**
5. The role play activity helped me to understand what I needed to learn
   **yes/no**
6. After the role play activity the teacher asked questions that made me think.
   **yes/no**
7. Some of the learning activities after the role play were difficult and challenging.
   **yes/no**
8. The lesson contained activities that kept me busy and interested all the time.
   **yes/no**
9. During the lesson the teacher regularly checked my understanding.
   **yes/no**
10. I would like the teacher to use role play again to help me learn.
    **yes/no**

**Thank you for completing this questionnaire**

---

This type of questionnaire can easily be adapted to gain feedback from learners that focus on the 'new' approach being taken in Unit 1 or the activity in Unit 2. It requires the learners to make a decision, a straight *yes* or *no* so means they can complete it in a few minutes at the end of a session to provide some immediate feedback.

The main disadvantage of using this type of checklist questionnaire is it doesn't tell us why a learner didn't enjoy taking part in the role play activity or why they found the learning activities after the role play difficult and challenging. To overcome this problem the next example allows the learners an opportunity to elaborate on their answers but it will take them longer to complete. To generate more ideas and discussion learners could complete it as part of a small group.

---

### LEARNER QUESTIONNAIRE

Please answer the questions as honestly as possible.

1. Was the start of the session interesting and did it gain your attention?                                      **yes/no**
   If the answer is yes, explain why. If the answer was no, explain why not.

   _____

2. Did you enjoy taking part in the role play activity?    **yes/no**
   If the answer is yes, explain why. If the answer was no, explain why not.

   _____

3. Did the role play activity help you understand what you needed to learn?                                      **yes/no**
   If the answer is yes, explain why. If the answer was no, explain why not.

   _____

4. In today's lesson were you kept busy and interested at all times?                                            **yes/no**
   If the answer is yes, explain why. If the answer was no, explain why not.

   _____

5. Would you like to use role play again to help you learn?                                                     **yes/no**
   If the answer is yes, explain why. If the answer was no, explain why not.

   _____

**Thank you for completing this questionnaire**

Learner feedback can also be obtained using structured interviews. A list of prepared questions is produced that focus on particular aspects of teaching, learning or aspects of the course being evaluated. This approach is normally used on a one-to-one basis and the learner's responses are recorded as they happen. Devising open questions such as *'What three activities did you learn most from in today's lesson and why?'* or *'How can the science lesson be made more interesting when we can't use the laboratory?'* enables us to use structured interviews to probe quite deeply. They can also be used in conjunction with questionnaires to gain feedback on specific issues a learner may have. However, we need to be aware that when a learner is being interviewed they may want to please the interviewer rather than give their honest opinions.

The technique of gathering learner feedback using a structured interview with a small or representative group of learners is often referred to as a 'focus group' and is gaining in popularity as educational institutions respond to what's euphemistically called the 'learner voice'. In this informal method the group of learners provide feedback responses in answer to prepared written and/or oral questions and their responses are followed up with a short discussion to clarify and complete the points they have made. It is most often used to provide feedback when evaluating a sequence of learning activities such as a module, study unit or topic. More often than not focus groups tend to avoid asking specific questions about learning and teaching, but to be effective it does need questions structured so they probe these often sensitive areas. This requires skilful management, particularly during any discussion time, as the learners need to be kept on task whilst at the same time trying to ensure they all participate and have a 'voice'. Notes of the discussion should be recorded and used to summarise feedback comments and the learners should be thanked for their time and effort.

The methods of obtaining learner feedback discussed so far normally take place at the end or at some time shortly after the end, of a lesson or series of lessons. To obtain more immediate feedback on any type of teaching or learning strategy being used in a lesson Race (2005: p. 225) advocates using Post-it notes to obtain what he calls 'fast feedback'. Asking learners to write on Post-it notes what they have learned at different stages during the session gives immediate feedback. The Post-it notes can then be displayed on the desk for the teacher to find out how the session is going. The Post-it notes could also be collected at the end of a session to find out what learners have learnt.

Race also suggests using the words 'stop', 'start', and 'continue' on a Post-it, as shown in the diagram below.

The teacher could ask the learners 'If I were to teach this class tomorrow with other people, what do you suggest I need to STOP *doing*, START *doing* and CONTINUE *doing?*'

The 'stop' entries are the things you don't want to hear but may need to hear. For example, 'STOP *talking for so long at the start of the session*', 'STOP *asking the same people all the questions*' or 'STOP *making us copy so many notes from the whiteboard*'.

The 'start' entries may give the teacher some ideas about what to do next time. The responses could include comments such as 'START *using more practical activities that make us think rather than write*', 'START *to give us time to think when answering a question*' or 'START *to slow down when demonstrating a new skill*'.

The 'continue' responses are what teachers like to hear and they are often surprising. For example, they may write 'CONTINUE *to use group work*', 'CONTINUE *taking us on study trips to interesting places*' or 'CONTINUE *to give us detailed feedback on our assignments*'.

Using this Post-it method will obviously throw up contradictions as some learners will want you to stop something while others will want you to continue the same things. This is where, over a period of time we will find out from learners what helps them to learn and what doesn't.

Another simple method of obtaining immediate learner feedback is to issue each learner in the class with an A4 laminated sheet. One side is coloured green, to indicate they are confident they know the answer to a question, and the other side is red to indicate they are not confident. This also ensures every learner must make a response when a question is asked by the teacher. Holding up the responses and seeing how many reds and green are on display is a quick visual way of obtaining simple feedback. If there are lots of reds the teacher must think immediately about the teaching and learning strategies s/he is using. Even more simple would be to ask the learners to place the cards on the desk, red side up to indicate they do not understand the question or concept or green side up to indicate they do.

Japanese car manufacturers have for many years used a system rather like the old 'suggestion box' where line workers submit their own views on how quality can be improved. In one year alone a Toyota factory received over 60,000 such responses of which 31,000 led to improvements. A similar feedback method could be used in your classroom where learners can 'post' any feedback they think will help improve their learning. These can of course be anonymous if the learner does not want their identity known.

Most teachers are comfortable with the concept of using learner feedback to evaluate courses and it is part of their regular practice. However, most are far more wary of using it to evaluate learning and teaching. They see any process of gaining learner feedback as being time-consuming and others confuse it with assessment outcomes. Most teachers would say that they can judge the success of learning activities by looking at the facial expressions of their learners. Yet, when experiments were conducted on this, teachers emerged as no more proficient in judging reactions than any other occupational group.

Our experience as teacher trainers working with teachers from all over the world that have used learner feedback to evaluate learning and teaching has been both positive and consistent. When teachers use it for the first time they are often pleasantly surprised by their learners' positive and supportive remarks. They are sometimes quite motivated by the feedback and many say that they will continue to use it as part of their reflective practice. Our feeling is that many teachers have been imaginative and resourceful in obtaining learner feedback. Teachers with young learners have developed some interesting strategies to gain feedback from their learners which include simple written statements/questions using 'smiley face' replies. Many also enlist the help of parents to help gain useful feedback from the very young learners. The Certificate for Teachers and Trainers programme gives teachers opportunities to make the 'learner voice' heard in more meaningful and constructive ways. Using different methods to obtain rigorous feedback from learners, and then analysing it as part of the evaluation process, can help to improve learning, teaching and all the other different aspects that go into what makes up a successful course.

## ASSESSMENT OUTCOMES

The results of assessment can tell you more than simply how well learners have achieved. They can also be used as an indicator of the effectiveness of the teaching. However, it would be unwise to take such data and assume, without careful analysis, that it is an accurate indicator of the quality of the teaching or the learning. For example, if a group of learners all passed a summative assessment, the teacher could assume the teaching and learning was effective. But this may not necessarily be the case. It could just as easily be assumed these learners were a particularly able and well motivated group who learned despite, rather than because of, the effectiveness of the teaching. On the other hand, if a teacher takes a group of learners who are struggling with the level of work and very few passed the summative assessment it would be wrong to automatically assume it was due to poor teaching. It could be the learners might need to be on a different programme to meet their current needs or the time allocated to deliver the programme was too short. It might even be the case that the summative assessment was not a valid or reliable test.

On-going (formative) assessment often provides teachers with a more reliable and timely measure of how well they are teaching and how well their students are learning. The formative assessment methods adopted may range from using directed open questioning, quizzes and games through to practice exams. The important point is that if just one or two learners give incorrect responses to a question, then it could be it is only those particular individuals who are having a problem grasping what is being taught. This can often be dealt with on a one-to-one or small group basis. However, if the majority of the learners failed to give the required answer the teacher needs to analyse the reasons for this, including the way the topic has been taught.

To evaluate if learning is taking place as a lesson progresses, any formative assessment methods being used are ideally combined with other types of feedback. For example, through observation of classroom activity a teacher can determine if all the learners are engaged in the learning process. They can also observe body language, how learners respond to questioning and what questions they ask. This may well provide the teacher with a more reliable indicator of how the session is succeeding and whether the students are learning, rather than just relying on the results of assessment outcomes

## REFLECTION

### KEEPING A REFLECTIVE JOURNAL

When we start to teach we often use the methods employed by the teachers who taught us. We learned and passed our exams using their methods – so they must be effective! But teaching and learning are complex and dynamic processes that we can never fully understand. We can't arrive at a 'final solution' that enables us to say 'that's how to do it'. The point was made in Section 1 that much of what we learn is from experience but we emphasised that doing the same thing over and over again, namely teaching, does not in itself guarantee we will learn and become better teachers. What needs to happen is that at some stage we need time for thinking and reflection so we do learn from our experiences. If this sounds familiar it is because once again we are using Kolb's learning cycle as our 'model' in trying to understand how people learn. If you return to Figure 6 on page 16 you will note that one way of helping us to reflect is to keep and maintain a Reflective Journal.

To be an effective reflective practitioner is a skill in itself and all teachers should be encouraged to keep and maintain a Reflective Journal to help develop that skill. It is common practice in many other professions such as medicine and law, and among professional sports people, artists and designers to keep a Reflective Journal as it is often difficult to recall what happened yesterday, never mind last week, last month or last year. Making a record of an event, no matter how short, enables us to look back and reflect on any particular lesson, approach, activity or experience, and think about or analyse what did or didn't work well.

## SELF EVALUATION

Some teachers initially find evaluating their own performance daunting but ultimately it will help to improve future practice. We have all taught lessons that have been ineffective and gone badly, no matter how experienced we are as teachers. The important thing is not to start apportioning blame either towards the learners, the resources, the management or yourself. Making a few notes immediately after the lesson in your Reflective Journal or on the lesson plan may be useful at this stage, but as busy people with possibly other classes to teach that day we need more time for reflection. An example of these initial few notes after teaching a group of 10-year-olds some basic number work could look as follows:

• Took ages to prepare a 20 minute PowerPoint demonstration but class generally noisy and continual poor behaviour from the 4 students who disrupt most lessons when teaching this group.

• Students stayed more on task when split into groups doing the matching games but with 30 in the class only had sufficient resources for 5 groups and a few of the quieter students only watched rather than participated.

- One of the two groups who finished the games first disturbed the other three groups so not all the students completed the tasks and not all the learning objectives were achieved.

Remember, the initial journal entries are there to remind you of some of the things that did or didn't go well in the lesson, this is the doing part of Kolb's learning cycle. You may decide to add further notes at a later stage before making time for reflection because it is inevitable that since teaching the lesson you would have had an 'internal' dialogue with yourself going through in more detail what went well in the lesson and what didn't. Those further journal entries could look something like this:

- The classroom is small for 30 students and the layout is traditional.
- Transferred OHT demonstration onto PowerPoint as I want to use more up-to-date equipment and then got the students to copy all the bullet-points into their exercise books.
- There is a wide range of ability in the class and whilst most of the students can answer direct questions correctly many fail to recognise the material when presented as part of a wider problem or in a practical context.
- The 4 students who disrupt each lesson always sit together and work in the same group.

When it comes to reflection, the reviewing part of Kolb's learning cycle, you will find it useful again to make notes in your Reflective Journal. The reflections on this lesson could look like this:

- Continue using PowerPoint to back up my demonstrations but I must make them shorter, maximum 5 minutes, and more visual, not just a list of bullet points.
- The class was motivated when doing the matching games in groups but I need to:
  - ➢ set the classroom out in cabaret style to promote group work
  - ➢ organise the groups so that early on the more able students can help the weaker ones

➢ ensure the 4 disruptive students are always working in different groups
➢ prepare worksheets so during the demonstration I can ask students questions instead of them doing lots of copying from the screen.

• Continue to use active learning methods such as games and role play to move the learners from the knowledge stage of Bloom's Taxonomy through to comprehension before doing any application.

• Prepare differentiated learning activities so that later in the lesson the groups can be re-organised to enable the more able learners to tackle harder analytical problems and allow me to work with the less able students to ensure they are ready to apply their knowledge and comprehension.

Most of the time this reflective practice is carried out in isolation but it can be more effective and rewarding when discussed with a colleague or mentor who is an experienced teacher and perhaps a subject specialist, even if they have not observed the lesson. This is the 'learning or abstract conceptualisation' stage of Kolb's learning cycle because hopefully, we have made the 'connections' that have given us some insight as to what we will do differently next time we teach this group or this topic.

Having reflected we now want to 'apply' our new learning, the final stage of Kolb's learning cycle. Pragmatically we may not be able to put into action immediately all the things we want to do differently next time but things like re-arranging the classroom and organising the groups for peer support, or using shorter PowerPoint demonstrations can be implemented with this group in the next lesson.

Keeping and maintaining a Reflective Journal is an important method of obtaining feedback that can be used for the analysis and evaluation of learning, teaching and the course programme. What hopefully we have demonstrated is that reflection and evaluation, like learning, is a continuous process. It is a cycle and never ends.

## ANALYSING THE FEEDBACK

Obtaining feedback in terms of data from all the different sources discussed is all well and good but it is only part of the evaluation process. It is of little use unless we reflect and carry out some meaningful analysis that enables us to make judgements about the quality of teaching and learning and the courses we teach, and this ultimately leads to improvements. The data comes in two forms, quantitative and qualitative.

Quantitative data is measured on a numerical scale and can be analysed using statistical methods. Most summative assessment data is quantitative, which means the results can then be presented in the form of tables, pictograms, charts, histograms and graphs. This makes analysis of the data easier when trying to make comparisons or spot trends. For example, we might conclude that the trend for the percentage of students achieving an A level pass in English Language over the past five years is steadily rising, or the percentage of students achieving a pass grade in GCSE History in 2008 is higher than in 2007.

Qualitative data is extremely varied but includes any information that can be captured that is not numerical in nature. The questionnaires used to obtain learner feedback shown on pages 115 and 116 are examples of qualitative data as they do not have any type of numbering system assigned to them. Qualitative data is still subjective even if we assign numerical values to questions as they are asking for opinions and not measurable facts. Even so, qualitative data often does have numbers applied to make any subsequent analysis easier and more manageable as illustrated in the following example.

---

LEARNER QUESTIONNAIRE

Please answer each of the statements using the following rating scale:

| **1** | **2** | **3** | **4** |
|---|---|---|---|
| **Strongly disagree** | **Disagree** | **Agree** | **Strongly agree** |

1. The introduction to today's lesson told me clearly what it was going to be about.

| **1** | **2** | **3** | **4** |
|---|---|---|---|

2. I knew throughout the lesson what I had to do.

| **1** | **2** | **3** | **4** |
|---|---|---|---|

3. The start of the lesson was interesting and gained my attention.

| **1** | **2** | **3** | **4** |
|---|---|---|---|

4. I enjoyed taking part in the role play activity.

| **1** | **2** | **3** | **4** |
|---|---|---|---|

5. The role play activity helped me to understand what I needed to learn.

| **1** | **2** | **3** | **4** |
|---|---|---|---|

6. After the role play activity the teacher asked questions that made me think.

| **1** | **2** | **3** | **4** |
|---|---|---|---|

7. Some of the learning activities after the role play were difficult and challenging.

| **1** | **2** | **3** | **4** |
|---|---|---|---|

8. The lesson contained activities that kept me busy and interested all the time.

| **1** | **2** | **3** | **4** |
|---|---|---|---|

9. During the lesson the teacher regularly checked my understanding.

| **1** | **2** | **3** | **4** |
|---|---|---|---|

10. I would like the teacher to use role play again to help me learn.

| **1** | **2** | **3** | **4** |
|---|---|---|---|

**Thank you for completing this questionnaire**

---

It is not uncommon for people to confuse feedback with evaluation. This is because teachers and trainers often get students or participants to complete 'evaluation questionnaires' or 'happy sheets' at the end of a course or a day's training and call it evaluation, but it isn't. Completion of the forms provides feedback as part of the much wider evaluation process. We have seen how a variety of feedback methods can be used from different sources to collate evidence and data but it is only after it has been analysed that any recommendations for improvements to the learning, teaching or course programme can be made.

In the Certificate for Teachers and Trainers course you are required to gather feedback from your learners, a colleague acting as a professional observer and any other sources you feel appropriate for the approach chosen for Unit 1, the activity chosen for Unit 2 and the experience chosen for Unit 3. The feedback is then analysed so judgements can be made on:

- *what learning outcomes* were achieved for the approach used in Unit 1 and the activity used in Unit 2, and *what were the main professional development outcomes* of the experience used in Unit 3
- *what were the practical professional outcomes experienced* in planning and preparing the approach used in Unit 1 and the activity used in Unit 2, and *what issues appear to have arisen* during the experience in Unit 3
- *how* you would *modify* your use of the approach in Unit 1, the activity in Unit 2 and the experience in Unit 3 to *make it more effective* the next time you use or try it.

In your institution you more than likely already have established feedback mechanisms in place. We are not asking you to re-invent the wheel but you might want to modify and or develop new ones that provide focused feedback to analyse and evaluate the approach chosen for Unit 1, the activity for Unit 2 and the experience for Unit 3.

## EVALUATION

At the outset we need to distinguish the difference between assessment and evaluation as the terms are sometimes confused when used in an educational context. We saw earlier how assessment can be considered as making judgements about a learner's learning progress, called formative or on-going assessment, or their learning achievement, called summative or final assessment. Evaluation is also about making judgements but in a much broader context because it involves making decisions on the effectiveness of:

- learning – assessment results are just one source of data used to analyse and evaluate students' learning
- professional practice – where we learn from experience through reflective practice to improve our teaching and learning skills
- courses – as well as teaching and learning there are lots of other aspects of a learning programme that can be evaluated such as the course structure, aims and objectives, learning materials and resources, facilities and equipment, assessment, organisation, documentation, learning outcomes, etc.

We also need to acknowledge that evaluation is part of the learning process and the best teachers use it to learn and improve their professional practice. Consider Figure 27 which illustrates how, in the context of the Certificate for Teachers and Trainers programme, after doing an activity we learn through reflective practice. We then use our 'new' learning, together with our existing knowledge and skills, to evaluate and make decisions on how to improve students' learning and our own professional practice.

In Units 1 and 2 you need to gain feedback from your learners and a colleague acting as a professional observer, together with notes from your Reflective Journal and any other feedback evidence you think relevant for analysis. The analysis must focus on what went well and what didn't in terms of the learning and practical professional (teaching) outcomes. You will then be in a position to make judgements and indicate how you would modify and suggest improvements to the activity to make it more effective the next time you use it. As the activity chosen for Unit 3 focuses on an experience away from the immediate learning environment, such as planning a scheme of assessment or working with another department, then the

How will you modify the approach chosen for Unit 1 and the activity chosen for Unit 2 to make it more effective the next time you use it?

How will you modify the experience chosen for Unit 3 to make it more effective the next time you try it?

Unit 1 develop a new teaching approach
Unit 2 facilitate active learning
Unit 3 reflection on practice

To assist in the reflective process arrange to obtain feedback from your learners for Units 1 and 2 and from peers for Unit 3. Feedback from a colleague acting as a professional observer must be obtained for all 3 Units. You should also keep a reflective journal or diary to record your thoughts as this will enable you to look back on what happened at the time as things are easily forgotten.

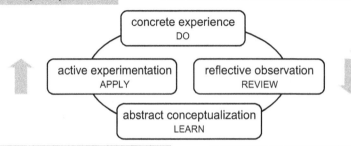

concrete experience
DO

active experimentation
APPLY

reflective observation
REVIEW

abstract conceptualization
LEARN

What *learning* outcomes were achieved from Units 1 and 2 and what were the *practical* professional outcomes you experienced in planning, preparing and using the approach or activity?

What were the main professional development outcomes *learned* from the experience in Unit 3 and what issues appear to have arisen during the experience?

How has each approach, activity and experience used helped to improve your understanding of learning and teaching to improve future practice.

Where possible set aside some time to meet with your learners to discuss what they felt about the new teaching approach and activities to facilitate active learning planned and managed in Units 1 and 2. Do the same with your peers for Unit 3.

Set aside sufficient time for more in-depth discussion with your observer based on their feedback report comments as part of a professional discussion

Use the feedback, together with any other relevant evidence or data, to reflect specifically on the approach, activity and experience used.

**Figure 27**: *Kolb's learning cycle applied to the Certificate*

analysis is based on feedback from a professional observer and the participants in the experience such as colleagues teaching on the same course, colleagues from a different department, specialist colleagues who deal with pastoral care and advice, parents, employers, etc. The analysis will enable you to identify what were the main professional development outcomes of the experience and what issues appear to you to have arisen during the experience. You will then be in a position to make judgements and indicate how you would modify and suggest improvements to the experience to make it more effective the next time you try it.

Evaluation is often the forgotten element in Kolb's learning cycle but we need to build it into our work from the outset. There is a real requirement to keep evaluation ongoing because:

- the process helps you to make judgements and indicate how you would modify and suggest improvements the next time you use or try out the activity
- it leads to more effective teaching and learning and you will be able to refine your learners' experiences and match their learning needs more closely
- learning is all about what learners do, and so getting feedback from them on the effectiveness of their learning activities is very important.

Think of evaluation like this. If car manufacturers do not constantly update their products in the light of rapidly changing customer needs then their share of the market would quickly fall. Teachers can only make their future teaching and learning activities more effective if they can reflect on and make use of their ongoing evaluation. This reinforces the concept that to be an effective teacher one must also be an effective learner. All of the evaluation data and information gathered from different sources will be of little use unless the teacher carries out some meaningful analysis and then uses their reflective practice skills to improve their own teaching practice and the students' learning.

The evaluation process linked with inspection, quality assurance and appraisal systems are very far reaching and involve a great deal of investment in terms of time and money.

We are dealing here much more with evaluation at the micro-level because it is only the chosen activity, and the impact it has had on both students' learning and your own professional practice, that is being evaluated. This methodology is familiar to other professionals such as doctors, lawyers and accountants who also use the concepts and practices involved in evaluation to improve their professional practice. In these professions, issues of accountability and quality assurance, which are second nature to most of us as teachers are now being increasingly formalized. In these senses the importance of evaluation in each Unit of the Certificate for Teachers and Trainers programme sets professional teaching practice in a modern context.

# SECTION 3

## OBSERVERS, COLLEAGUES AND TRAINERS

## SESSION OBSERVATION

We keep emphasising that the best teachers are always keen and willing to learn and the best way of learning is by doing or from experience. This means the more we teach the better our professional knowledge and skills should become. But we know this isn't always the case because unless we have time to reflect on what we do the more likely it is we will carry on with our existing practice: good, bad or indifferent. We discussed in Section 3 how keeping a Reflective Journal can help us to recall significant events that have occurred both inside and outside the classroom and which at a later date can remind us of what happened so we can learn from the experience. But trying to learn on our own in this way is often difficult and not always very effective. This is where receiving critically constructive feedback of our practice from a professional observer such as a mentor, colleague, manager or teacher trainer can help.

Many teachers find the most valuable part of any teacher training programme is the feedback they receive from an observed lesson. It is one of the few opportunities they get to reflect on current practice with the support of a colleague who can help to identify what went well in a particular lesson and what could be improved. As a practice-based qualification the Certificate for Teachers and Trainers programme places a great deal of emphasis on candidates obtaining feedback from a colleague acting as a professional observer for each of the three different activities they are required to undertake. Their role in the teacher's development as a reflective practitioner is crucial and they must know what they are looking for and the approach to take for each activity. It is normal practice for an observer to make notes and record both general and specific points when observing a lesson. The CIE OBSERVATION RECORD form uses a common format, no matter what the context, which is then used as the basis for a professional dialogue during the feedback session.

So who should act as the professional observer and what should they be looking for in the different activities? When experimenting using a new teaching and learning approach, as required in Unit 1, the professional observer could be:

- an experienced colleague from the same curriculum area who is a qualified teacher
- a mentor who is an experienced and qualified teacher
- a qualified teacher trainer who is familiar with your role as a teacher
- a manager who will act in a supportive rather than a judgemental role.

It is important the observer is aware not only of the learning aims and objectives of the session being observed but how the teacher is attempting to change and improve their practice. This means the feedback must focus on the key processes of both teaching and learning and how *active learning* is being *facilitated*. The most useful and instructive observations come about when the professional observer acts as a 'critical friend' and indicates not only what went well in the lesson, but what didn't go so well. As part of the professional dialogue, which normally takes place some time after the lesson to leave time for reflection, the observer should discuss and make suggestions as to how the new approach being adopted can be further developed and improved.

## THE PRAISE SANDWICH APPROACH

A useful feedback technique adopted by many experienced observers is based on what's commonly known as a 'praise sandwich' approach. The observer starts the feedback session with some praise of what went well or was effective in the activity. This is followed by some constructive criticism that points to not only what didn't go well, but more importantly, makes suggestions as to how to improve future practice. The observer then concludes with some further praise. This technique may be used on a number of occasions during the feedback session as different phases of the lesson are discussed.

Using the praise sandwich approach let's take the example of a teacher called Deanna who is in her second year of teaching. As part of her timetable Deanna teaches a class of 18 mixed ability and mixed gender 16-year-old learners studying Life Skills. The session to be observed is a two hour lesson on how to cook a themed fish dish. Mainly due to the lack of planning time and being fairly new to teaching Deanna taught the same lesson last year by showing the students a video of a well known chef cooking a fish dish. She then got them to individually select a theme and write an assignment on how they would prepare and cook the dish. This year her approach is to start the lesson with a practical demonstration and then get the students to work in small groups to discuss various themes before they individually cook a chosen dish with vegetables. In the same lesson 3 weeks ago Deanna had taken the students to a nearby market to learn about the different types of vegetables and fish available locally. The students had clearly enjoyed the educational visit so in this lesson she planned for the students to do some practical work and use both experiences to help them write their assignment.

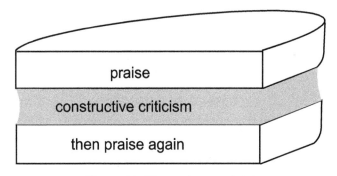

**Figure 28**: *The praise sandwich*

Deanna has asked a colleague, who is a qualified teacher trainer and an experienced practitioner, to observe the two hour lesson. She met with the observer for 30 minutes two days before the lesson took place to briefly discuss the learning needs of the group and how they were progressing in their learning. At the meeting Deanna also shared with her observer the scheme of work and the lesson plan, which identified the following learning aim and objectives for the session:

---

**Aim** – Create a themed fish dish with vegetables
**Objectives** – The learners will be able to:
- select a theme for cooking the dish
- prepare the fish and vegetables ready for cooking
- cook the fish and vegetables according to the selected theme
- serve the themed fish dish with vegetables
- create a list of criteria to evaluate the themed fish dish
- evaluate the themed fish dish using the agreed criteria.

---

Deanna used the pre-meeting to explain how this time she has planned to use more active learning methods because in last year's lesson the group being taught clearly became bored watching a 30 minute video. As a result they became very de-motivated when required to produce their written assignment. The observer was supplied with blank copies of the CIE OBSERVATION RECORD form and Deanna arranged for the feedback session to take place two days after the lesson was taught. Whilst it is often common practice to give immediate lesson feedback Deanna felt it was better for both her and the observer to have some time to reflect on how the lesson went. It would also ensure the professional discussion would focus on the new approach being taken and how learning was being facilitated. A copy of the CIE OBSERVATION RECORD form completed by the observer is shown below.

### OBSERVATION RECORD

| **Name of activity:** Practical work | |
|---|---|
| **Date of activity:** Tuesday, 12 May 2009 | **Location of activity:** San Antonio Study Centre |
| **Name of observer:** Natalie Rodriguez-Diez | **Job title of observer:** Teacher Trainer |
| **Name of Certificate candidate:** Deanna García Ramírez | |

---

**Highlights of the activity**

General comment: Starting the session by sharing the lesson aim and objectives and then linking back to the students' visit to the local market quickly gained the learners' interest and made them eager to learn.

The practical work was well organised and allowed you to give 1:1 support to both the weaker and more able learners as and when required. This clearly demonstrated differentiated learning taking place as the learners were allowed to progress at their own pace. Encouraging peer support during the practical work and then at the end involving the learners in assessing each other's work and giving feedback were also further examples of differentiated active learning taking place.

The lesson was well planned and all the resources were available when required. This helped the flow of the lesson and ensured a smooth transistion beween activities. The approach using practical work allowed you to facilitate more active learning than in previous lessons. It was evident the learners were engaged in the learning process throughout the majority of the lesson and most of the learning objectives were achieved.

Specific points: Before starting the demonstration you ensured all the students could see the preparation area. All explanations were clear and your enthusiasm for the subject kept the learners motivated and interested throughout the lesson.

All health and safety issues were identified and constantly reinforced throughout the session. However, when similar practical work approaches are being used in future lessons I would suggest they should be acknowledged by incorporating them into the learning objectives.

**Points for development by candidate**

General comment: The learners were not always entirely clear what was expected of them as the demonstration at the start of the lesson, which lasted just under 30 minutes, was too long. This meant there was too much information for most of them to remember at any one time. Instead, consider breaking a skills demonstration down into more manageable stages or 'chunks of learning'. Also, don't be afraid to let a learner carry out a stage of the demonstration (under your supervision) and encourage them to verbalise what they are doing and why. This leaves you free to use directed open questioning so that all the learners can be involved in the activity, even the shy learners.

Make sure sufficient time is left to properly conclude the lesson so student learning is checked and reinforced

---

Specific points: Greater use of directed open questioning should be made to challenge the learners' knowledge and understanding. They also need to be given more thinking time so when asked a question; don't expect an answer immediately, give some 'wait time. When a learner answers a question correctly just say 'thank you' and continue to ask the question to other learners, this keeps them thinking and allows you to follow up with more probing questions such as 'Can you explain why' or 'Give me an example', etc.

All learners bring existing experiences to the classroom so use them to make the learning more relevant. You could also consider incorporating into the written assignment some differentiated activities that involve the learners working out the cost of the meal and doing some research into environmental issues associated with the fishing industry and energy consumption.

---

| **Signature:** | Print name: Natalie Rodriguez-Diez | Date: 12/5/09 |

The main purpose of any OBSERVATION RECORD form is that it is used as the basis of a professional discussion between the teacher and an observer as part of an evaluation process. Judgements on the learning outcomes achieved and the practical professional outcomes experienced in planning, preparing and using the new teaching and learning approach can then be made. The completed form should be detailed enough to record the significant highlights and points for development which the observer wants to discuss in much greater detail during the feedback session. This is why an observer needs to be an experienced supportive colleague who does not try to record everything that happens in a lesson but keeps focused on how the approaches to teaching and learning facilitate active learning. We have already discussed and given examples of typical forms or checklists observers might use in Section 2 and it was stressed that the focus of the observation should be on the learners and their learning. This means the emphasis is more on what the students are doing rather than on what the teacher is doing. To help keep this focus an observer might ask the following questions when attempting to make judgements on how an approach or use of an activity is facilitating active learning:

Did the learners:

- participate in learning activities suitable for all of them whatever their age, ability or experience?
- find the learning activities demanding for the range of abilities within the class?
- find the learning activities motivating and relevant so they aroused curiosity?
- make suitable progress in the learning activities to achieve all or most of the learning objectives?
- participate in activities that challenged them, including the more able learners?
- make relevant spontaneous comments, ask questions, engage in debate, offer ideas?
- show a keen interest in the tasks planned for them?
- have pride in their work, understand the concepts of what they have learned and are eager to explain what they are doing and why?
- interact productively as they were learning?
- have their interest engaged and sustained throughout the lesson?
- all participate in the lesson and keep on task?
- have activities that developed and applied knowledge and skills?
- have tasks that were challenging and promoted deep rather than surface learning?
- have their learning and work in progress constantly checked and corrected?
- take sufficient responsibility for their own learning no matter what their ability?

It is also worth mentioning that in any lesson observation the observer as well as the teacher will learn a great deal from the experience.

When looking in greater detail at the process of facilitating active learning, as required in Unit 2, a teacher might just use one or several observers over a period of time to give feedback on the approaches being developed. If several observers are used each one should complete an OBSERVATION RECORD form so the feedback can be used to evaluate the learning and teaching outcomes of the activity. If the same observer is used throughout the process it is likely they will complete more than one OBSERVATION RECORD form and give feedback at appropriate intervals. The skills and experience of any professional observer invited to provide feedback on the facilitation of active learning in Unit 2 will be similar to those outlined for the observation in Unit 1 and the completion of the OBSERVATION RECORD form will also be similar.

In Unit 3 the activity looks in greater detail at a teacher's involvement in aspects of professional development beyond the teaching/learning context and away from the immediate learning environment. The focus of the activity is on the ways and means of developing one's thinking about the critical awareness of the practice of teaching and training and this means the observer's involvement will be more informal. Working with and using an experienced colleague who can meet as and when necessary often provides the most effective feedback for this activity. They will still complete one or more of the CIE OBSERVATION RECORD forms to use as the basis for the professional discussions to gain feedback for evaluation purposes. No matter what activity is chosen for Unit 3 it still requires preparation and planning, putting into action and then reviewing and evaluating. If this process sounds familiar it is because it is describing a learning experience. Learning to teach is no different to any other learning experience so again we could use Kolb's experiential learning cycle to model our practice.

## EXAMPLE OF A UNIT 3 ACTIVITY USING KOLB'S CYCLE

The example shown in Figure 29 would be relevant for a Unit 3 activity as it involves a teacher working with colleagues from another department to develop joint programmes of study.

Managing change is rarely easy and managing the change of your own teaching practice is even more challenging but

To improve future practice:
- some of the maths concepts will be taught by the science teachers as part of a science topic
- if the timetabling of classes cannot be changed this academic year proposals for a joint approach between departments will made for next year
- the project team will now focus on how ICT can support differentiated learning in both subjects
- learner feedback during this course will focus on how the group is coping with the learning activities in both subjects

As a maths teacher I have been working with three colleagues from the science department developing joint programmes of study. The aim is for learners to understand and apply the mathematical concepts that underpin the science curriculum. We meet for 1 hour twice a week and so far the 30 week project has focused on designing schemes of work that complement each other. In doing so we are trying to ensure relevant mathematical concepts have been covered before tackling the science topics they support.

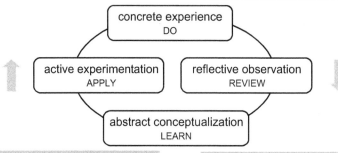

We are now 10 weeks into the project and I have learned:
- despite detailed planning some mathematical concepts could not be covered in the maths lessons before science colleagues needed to start a complementary topic.
- there is a wide range of abilities in the group and some students have significant 'gaps' in their learning so are finding both subjects difficult.
- timetabling of classes by different departments has not supported the collaborative approach
- ICT is not used in either the science or maths classes to support learning

After each meeting I make notes in my Reflective Journal of how the experience is progressing. I also regularly make reflective notes after each maths lesson.

As part of the reflective process I have asked an experienced colleague from the IT department to be an Observer and attend the weekly meetings. She provides feedback to the team every 5 weeks using the CIE Observation Record form.

My three science colleagues also provide feedback on the project including how the learners are progressing in their studies.

**Figure 29**: *Kolb's learning cycle with Unit 3 activity applied*

as Petty (2009) says 'You can't improve your teaching without changing it'. This is where the support of professional observers, colleagues and trainers observing what happens inside and outside the classroom is so vital in helping us to change and improve our professional teaching practice. We have seen how in a lesson it is fairly straightforward to make judgements on the 'performance' of a teacher and their teaching skills, but making a judgement on whether effective learning is taking place requires far more skill and experience. Therefore, choosing a professional observer to provide the kind of rigorous critical feedback required to evaluate learning and teaching is crucial if we want to continuously improve our practice to help our learners learn more effectively.

# SECTION 4

## PROCESSES IN DEVELOPING AN ACTIVITY

## CHOICE OF ACTIVITY

This involves a degree of reflection. It is a good idea to think about what in your current teaching-learning practice you would like to change or develop and then plot a way forward for this change. There are several scenarios surrounding this choice. You might feel that your teaching methods are in a rut, that you are merely repeating what you have always done and you want a way out of this to refresh both you and your learners. This state of affairs can all too easily arise and persist in teaching. It could be that you have a way forward but need some structure or even an excuse to try it out. You might be experimenting with different methods already but have no framework in which to share your experiences and findings. It might be that you have had in-service training in many spheres of educational activity but would like to get back to the heart of the matter – developing learning.

The Certificate can help you structure your own approach to the improvement of your own professional practice and you will receive some training from your Centre to help you along. The qualification itself is designed around three Units of study, each of which contains six optional approaches from which you will choose one. Thus your total assignment submission will comprise THREE approaches. The 'menu' of options has been constructed to cover most worthwhile avenues of development, so please do not cast around trying to make up new categories of your own! It is a good idea to look through all three Units and plot yourself a sequence of activities which you think best suits your own particular professional needs.

The Certificate itself was designed to offer a series of challenges to practising teachers. In the word 'challenge' there are a bundle of ideas which need a little more understanding. These include:

### 1. Risk

The notion of 'risk' seems fundamental to much human activity, though we tend to think in extremes such as climbing mountains, extreme sports and of course space travel. Many people do not feel fulfilled unless they have proved themselves against uncertainty and you would not get very far in business if you did not risk capital in search of profit. You could argue that much creative work sits at the edge of risk. Impressionist painters in France were ridiculed when their work was first exhibited. Some of Wagner's operas were openly jeered. Luis Bunuel was all but exiled from Spain for his movies. Yet it is not only a case of 'to boldly go' but also 'who dares wins', for wouldn't we be the poorer without Francis Bacon's tortured paintings which demonstrated once and for all that it was not just beauty which could spring out of oil painting? Or Vivienne Westwood's revolutionary designs which took fashion into a new dimension? Development of any kind incurs risk. We are in the same position in our own field of teaching and learning.

2. **An informed choice**

In the Certificate we are asking teachers to make a useful (to them) choice of Unit activities or approaches. Clearly most science teachers use practical work in some shape or form so simply selecting Approach A practical work in Unit 1 would not be a very adventurous move and ICT teachers would obviously be best advised to avoid Approach B in the same Unit. The Certificate syllabus contains further notes to help you make your choice.

3. **Outcomes**

We urge teachers not to get too attached to the outcomes of the activities they design and implement. It may well be that the activity you tried disappointed you in some way. Perhaps you made mistakes. Perhaps the learners did not respond. Perhaps you had to modify your plan as your learners took you in a different direction. These things happen to all of us. Examiners need to read about what happened and, more importantly your analysis of the problems and how you are going to take the situation forward in your next design. This is how we as teachers learn.

## DESIGN OF ACTIVITIES

We have already talked about the concept of 'Design' in Section 2 but a little more needs to be said about this in practical, Certificate based, terms.

1. **The design as a whole**

   There is no right or wrong way to work up a design for a Certificate activity. Some teachers like to set up their aims and objectives and work towards learning outcomes through learning activities which yield the desired outcomes. This is fine but it is not the only way to think about the learning session. Some teachers think of themselves as their learners and see the learning session as a set of experiences out of which will come outcomes which can then be related to objectives. This method may seem odd but does 'get under the skin' of learning. Yet others are very 'outcome driven' in their design thinking. Again there is no harm done in this approach. Maybe we ought to think more about how we know learning has taken place and what exactly did the learner take away from the learning session?

2. **Design content**

   In our experience teachers tend to give scant attention to *three* fundamental design considerations:

   ➤ Assessment

   We know that Formative Assessment (assessment for learning) is a vital and on-going part of our teaching work. We need to answer the question 'How do we know that learning has taken place?' Our designs should cater for this consideration.

   ➤ Evaluation

   Many well conceived plans say little or nothing about evaluation yet we know that without it we cannot complete the Kolb experiential cycle. We need to see what kind of evaluation will be taking place, who will be carrying it out, how and when.

> ➢ Design perils
> We would urge designers to be aware of two design problems. Firstly listing too many objectives which overloads content and pressurises time. It is better to have fewer objectives which can allow learners to relax into activities and for formative assessment and evaluation to be effective. Secondly you will need to consider two kindred notions – flexibility and back-up. Have you alternative methods and material if there is an electricity failure? What happens if you need to follow up an interesting point raised by a learner?

## PRACTICE – WHAT HAPPENED?

What did the learners and/or teachers actually do in the learning session or the professional activity (Unit 3)? This needs spelling out in your assignment. Between them the writers have observed many hundreds of learning sessions and we would urge teachers to learn from observation of other teachers and trainers in action. When observing, an experienced observer will always look at the learners. What are they supposed to be doing? What were they told to do? Do they need further support or guidance? Are they stimulated by the task? Are they working with enjoyment and interest? Their involvement and interest will say much about the way in which the session design is working out in practice. This sensing of how learning has taken place is at the very heart of our work as teachers. Really skilled teachers can perceive when support is needed and can encourage learners as the session progresses. They may be similarly attuned to the progress of meetings and presentations. Their skills in empathy, management of the 'flow' of activities are to be admired.

In our experience as learners when we were at school, college or on a training course we might have come across what we would consider as 'inspirational teachers'. It is very difficult to define such a person in professional terms, but we might suggest some of their characteristics – and don't be modest, you probably have some of these yourself! Characteristics include:

- Ability to create and sustain a 'warm' learning atmosphere in which learners feel they have ready and easy access to teacher support. Teacher is enthusiastic about content and understanding and can communicate that enthusiasm with humour and energy.

- Teacher has excellent knowledge of learner interests and skills and can make use of them in the learning session.

- Learners feel that the lessons are fun and feel they can try out ideas in class, knowing that the teacher will not ridicule them if they make mistakes.

- Teacher has a consistently positive approach to learning such that learners feel they are being valued and working towards really high standards.

- Teacher is not afraid to appear distinctive, even eccentric in preferences and opinions, challenging existing norms and orthodoxies.

There is no one personality type which marks out inspirational teachers, indeed they flourish in their diversity but they are all creative designers of learning situations and are able to encourage learners to develop their own skills and views. Why not use the Certificate's challenges to develop your own inspirational side?

## FEEDBACK

The concept of feedback is well understood in education but its use in practice is very much less in evidence. Teachers see themselves as busy individuals with many demands on their time and so gaining feedback is very often seen as a time consuming 'add on' or something reserved for more formal observation events. Essentially there are four ways of gaining feedback on your own professional practice.

1. Formal appraisal and other reviews of practice with senior colleagues including external inspection
2. Observation of classroom and other practice
3. Learner Feedback
4. Self Appraisal.

It is good practice to undertake a blend of all four types but individual circumstances will affect their frequency of use. Feedback is important because it acts as primary evidence in evaluation. So it is important to look at a range of feedback sources and analyse the feedback material so that the main points arising from it can be clarified and put into use. To be really useful, feedback needs to be carefully targeted otherwise it will be couched in general terms and thus be useless. It is much better to ask a few questions on specific points rather than a range of ideas which remain largely unexplored. Incidentally this advice holds for all four of the feedback methods identified above. Furthermore the operation of feedback needs to be an integral part of your Learning Programme Design and, where necessary, your Learning Session Design.

Merely collecting feedback is not enough. It needs to be analysed, either quantitatively (using simple statistical methods such as charts, measures such as means, medians and modes) or qualitatively highlighting recurrent views, typical responses or anomalous ideas. This information is almost priceless. There may be a great difference between what you thought went well in class and how your learners reacted. Many Certificate candidates are able to write intelligently about what happened in a learning session but are much less willing to look at the implications of feedback analysis including notes made from discussions with Observers. This makes it difficult for them to complete and use the Kolb teaching-learning cycle.

# EVALUATION

Almost the Cinderella of educational practice, the whole business of Evaluation remains a mystery for many teachers who (a) confuse it with Assessment, and (b) cannot see the point in it anyway! This may seem like a caricature of what goes on but like many such spikey observations there is more than a grain of truth in it. Feedback and Assessment are Evidence for Evaluation. Evaluation is a much bigger set of processes which will make statements about what has happened and recommendations for what could be – or needs to be – done in the future.

Evaluation can be frequent or infrequent, formal or informal. It can be carried out by the individual in the first place, say at an analytical stage, but it is almost always more worthwhile when shared with a colleague or observer or as part of a larger group, say departmental, review.

Framing evaluation is usually seen in terms of success or failure. 'This worked well so we will do that again in the next programme.' Many teachers relate the expected to the observed in their evaluation. 'They didn't see the value of this practical work.' Not infrequently evaluation slides into a list of negative statements, 'misfires' and resultant wish lists. This misses several important points. In the first place it may fail to isolate the very real progress being made by some learners ('value added') and in the second it may ignore vital considerations such as maturation, motivation and learner needs. Indeed it may simply be emphasising teaching rather than learning. Development of learning is the heart of our business as teachers. Evaluation should have this as its primary aim. This is why learner feedback and interaction with learners including informal chats is so precious for the development of learning. Teachers remote from their learners' interests and aspirations are unlikely to initiate intrinsic motivation and the ability to feed back useful ideas and their evaluation of learning will remain at a functional, factual level.

# SECTION 5

## NOTES ON UNIT ACTIVITIES

# INTRODUCTORY NOTES

Each of the 3 units of study offers a choice of six activities and you must choose and carry out ONE activity for each unit. As a reminder the units are:

UNIT 1: DEVELOPING A NEW TEACHING APPROACH
UNIT 2: FACILITATING ACTIVE LEARNING
UNIT 3: REFLECTING ON PRACTICE.

The following notes can be used as a guide to help you think about how each of the chosen 3 activities can help to improve your professional practice and your learners' learning. All of the illustrations have stemmed from actual teacher's day-to-day practice in a variety of contexts. We hope you find them useful and informative.

# UNIT 1: DEVELOPING A NEW TEACHING APPROACH

This unit is about the teacher developing a teaching approach they have not used before to facilitate active learning. Candidates should be encouraged to experiment and take 'risks' such that their thinking about teaching and learning is challenged. At the same time they need to be reassured that they need not worry if the 'new' approach is not entirely successful. However, what is important is they reflect on and evaluate the approach using learner and observer feedback to learn and to inform what might change in future practice.

## APPROACH A — PRACTICAL WORK

All teachers use practical work in their day-to-day teaching in a variety of forms. What needs to be thought about here is how it can be used to teach a topic that is normally taught using a more didactic teacher-led method such as a lecture or teacher demonstration. For example, students are often subjected to a lecture on the theory of Ohm's Law when being taught the basic concepts of electricity. A more practical approach, and one that promotes active learning, would be to get the students to wire up a simple circuit and then take a series of readings to 'discover' the relationship between the voltage, current and resistance. By devising a series of activities backed up with questions that make the students think, most, if not all of them, will be able to explain in their own words the relationship between voltage, current and resistance and then derive the formula that connects them.

Many teachers think they do not have to spend as much time planning a practical skills lesson as they do a theory lesson. This is a false premise, so teachers who select this activity have an opportunity to review and try a different approach to their established practice. For example, when teaching a simple skill such as planting a flower bulb in a pot, a teacher's established practice might be to demonstrate the skill to the whole class before getting them to practice it. An alternative approach could be for the teacher to get a student to do the demonstration or use pair work so they can 'experiment' to master the skill. This more 'experiential' approach, where students are learning from their mistakes, requires a great deal of planning to ensure all the learning objectives or competences are achieved. It also sometimes throws up some real creative thinking by students as they strive to develop their skills with limited or no experience. More complex skills should be taught by breaking them down into a chain of steps so that each step is learned separately. Each step is then practised until mastered to the required standard before 'chaining' them together to make up the complete skill.

Using a 'new' approach to practical work can also get teachers to think about whether they predominantly use deductive or inductive approaches to learning. In a deductive approach the teacher gives the students a general statement (or law) and then gets them to carry out activities that will confirm or verify the statement. In an inductive approach the teacher gets the students to carry out activities that will lead them to arrive at a generalised statement (or law). The two different approaches can be demonstrated using the following examples:

| TOPIC | DEDUCTIVE APPROACH | INDUCTIVE APPROACH |
|---|---|---|
| Magnetic forces | • Teacher states 'Only some metals are attracted by magnets'.<br><br>• Students given a range of objects made from different materials to test which are attracted by the magnets and confirm general statement. | • Teacher gives students a range of objects made from different materials.<br>• Students experiment with the objects to see which are attracted by the magnets and conclude with a general statement. |
| Mixing colours | • Teacher informs students that mixing the primary colours yellow and blue will make green.<br><br>• Students mix colours to test and confirm statement. | • Teacher gives the students a range of primary colours and asks them to make green.<br>• Students experiment by mixing together primary colours. |
| Interview skills | • Teacher lists process of do's and don'ts when interviewing.<br>• Students practice interview skills by videoing role play.<br><br>• Teacher plays back video and discusses the do's and don'ts of interviewing. | • Students use role play to interview each other.<br>• Students design interview guidelines in terms of do's and don'ts.<br>• Students re-interview each other using new guidelines. |

When you really think about it, most topics taught 'theoretically' can be taught using practical work. Activities that get students to measure lengths, construct models, perform tasks, demonstrate skills, create posters, play games, etc., rather than listen to a lecture, copy notes from a screen or watch a DVD should be encouraged.

## APPROACH B — USE OF ICT

The emphasis using this approach is how ICT supports students' learning and the remit is far wider than just you and your learners developing computer skills such as using word-processing, spreadsheets, databases or PowerPoint to present information. A good deal of time will be spent by the teacher at the design and planning stage carrying out research to find suitable software packages or websites that students can access as well as making sure equipment such as digital cameras, video cameras or even mobile phones are available when required. Planning time may also be spent developing ICT related differentiated tasks and activities designed to give all learners early success and ensure the more able students are 'stretched' and challenged in their thinking. If well designed, activities using ICT can involve lots of group work and peer teaching as they are strategies that promote student autonomy and encourages them to take responsibility for their own learning.

The Internet is clearly a powerful ICT resource students can use to research most topics, even from a young age, as part of a project or assignment. For example, if a group of learners were using the theme of *'People in the Past – The History of Egypt'* as part of a cross curriculum activity they could find out and learn how ancient Egyptians prepared food by accessing websites such as the BBC Learning Zone at *www.bbc.co.uk/ learningzone/clips/how-did-the-ancient-egyptians-prepare-food.* This does not mean that traditional resources such as the use of library text and reference books, newspapers, magazines, etc, should be abandoned in favour of solely using ICT, particularly when using 'closed' searches that requires the learners to look for specific information. The number of internet websites students can potentially access for information on any particular topic using search engines such as Google or Yahoo is often overwhelming, so teachers need to think carefully about how they are going to develop their own and their students' search skills.

If you are a teacher that has so far avoided using ICT as a teaching and learning strategy then selecting this approach will give you an ideal opportunity to 'experiment' and use it to develop your own, and more importantly, your students' ICT skills. If you already use ICT then trying a 'new' teaching and learning approach could focus on developing active learning tasks that involve the learners using some new software or accessing websites that have relevant and often interactive learning materials available. Suitable websites include media organisations such as the BBC, Teachers TV, national newspapers and magazines, museums, government departments, commercial companies, etc. There is also a great deal of free software made available to education organisations that is often worth investigating ranging from computer aided design to examination revision packages that most students find fun to use.

## APPROACH C — EDUCATIONAL VISIT

Teachers often underestimate the power of educational visits and the impact they can have on students' learning. When using this approach the teacher will again need to spend a good deal of time planning the visit and devising activities the students will be required to carry out before, during and after the visit. This means the visit needs to have clear learning aims and objectives with activities devised to meet those aims and objectives.

Educational visits can also provide opportunities for collaboration with colleagues who teach different subjects. Students often find it difficult to see the relationship between separately taught subjects in a holistic context. Visiting museums, art galleries, zoos, places of historical interest, industrial and commercial companies, etc, can help do this. Another great advantage of educational visits is the potential involvement of experts and employees who work in the establishment being visited and the fresh approach they often bring to learning. Involving them at the planning and all subsequent stages of the visit can give real added value to the learning experience.

Organising visits to museums, exhibitions, historical sites, etc., often allows students to get more 'hands-on' experience than most company visits due to health and safety issues. Sometimes students may view such venues as 'boring' so the teacher should try to spark their interest before the visit by outlining all the planned activities and then start the visit with something that grabs their attention. As well as teacher devised learning materials these venues often provide a wide range of their own resources which may need to be adapted to meet the required learning outcomes. Using the expertise of people who work at the venue should also be maximised. However, this doesn't mean the teacher 'hands over' responsibility of the learning to them but instead demonstrates to the students it is a collaborative exercise with the teacher fully involved.

No matter what venue students are visiting, activity sheets should be designed to challenge their thinking and get them to ask questions rather than simply answering a series of questions by ticking boxes. This is where visits lend themselves to differentiated learning activities. Students could also take photos, shoot video footage, draw sketches, etc., (with suitable permission) that can subsequently be used for displays and/or presentations of their learning.

## APPROACH D – ROLE PLAY/SIMULATION

Teachers who are reluctant to use role play are often pleasantly surprised at not only its effectiveness for learning but also the fun and enjoyment most students get out of participating in the activities, even the shy ones. Role play can be used by students in a variety of ways to learn. For example, a very simple role play is to get students to play the part of an atom in matter which involves them moving apart or bunching up together to demonstrate in a very simple way the difference between a solid and a liquid. Perhaps the most common use of role play is to try and change students' attitudes as well as develop their knowledge and skills. Acting out a health and safety scenario where somebody has been electrocuted often has a powerful effect on students as they realise their actions or inactions could ultimately lead to someone suffering a serious or fatal injury. Role play can be used in a wide variety of contexts such as:

- students taking on the role of significant historical figures or characters in a novel and then being interviewed by the other students regarding their actions, motives, etc.
- students acting out how shop assistants, taking different attitudes, deal with an irate customer returning faulty goods
- students take on the role of a hotel receptionist taking a booking over the telephone from a customer using a foreign language
- students prepare election addresses as candidates for different political parties and are then questioned by the other students acting as voters
- students produce menu cards and adverts to launch a new restaurant.

These examples illustrate how role play can be effective at any academic level and can be adapted to accommodate a wide variety of demands and detail. At the low end of Bloom's Taxonomy they are useful for identifying people's names, places and sequencing of events. At the higher end they help to develop a greater understanding and interpretation of events and attitudes as well as developing reasoning, analysis and evaluation skills as part of any decision making process.

Using simulation software enables students to 'experiment' and find solutions to problems that would often be difficult and dangerous to try out in normal circumstances. Simulation software is also useful for fault diagnosis where for example a teacher deliberately wires up a dangerous electrical circuit and the students are required to find the safe solution. Simulation also lends itself to peer teaching and working collaboratively to learn.

Both role play and simulation are approaches to teaching and learning that involve a high degree of student participation but they can be very time consuming to set up and administer. The role of the teacher is to facilitate learning and they must be prepared to hand over a certain amount of control to the students.

## APPROACH E — DISCUSSION AND DEBATE

What's the difference between a discussion and a debate? Put simply, a discussion is where all students are actively involved in talking to each other to solve problems, explore issues or take decisions, with the teacher managing but not dominating the situation. A debate is very similar to a discussion but tends to have more rules regarding procedure and is used when there is no right or wrong answer but allows both sides to explore different points of view. It is also managed more by the students than the teacher but fewer of them are actively involved.

A discussion often occupies only part of a lesson and may or may not require previous research. When covering a topic such as energy, the teacher might plan at some stage in the lesson for the students to discuss different types of energy sources and their impact on the environment. As this topic is often in the media students usually have enough background knowledge to make valuable contributions. Planning for a discussion to take place after showing a DVD or video is another technique used by teachers to ensure the students' attention stays focused throughout the programme as well as reinforcing learning. Using a discussion before, during and/or after a skills demonstration is another effective technique used to engage learners in the process.

If we continue with the theme of energy, a teacher could plan for the students to take part in a debate on the use of nuclear energy to generate electricity. In this more structured approach either the teacher nominates a chairperson or the students elect one. The students are then given time to do some research before debating the issues to an agreed procedure. This means not all the students may have the opportunity to participate in the debate itself. The teacher should only intervene in the process if the ground rules are not being adhered to. Using debates is an excellent strategy for getting students to consider two or more sides of any argument whether it is political, social, economic, technical, environmental, scientific, etc.

## APPROACH F — VISITING SPEAKER

Using a visiting speaker often helps in motivating students to learn due to the relevant and up-to-date experience they can bring to a particular topic. The speaker should be well briefed about the course, the students and where they are in their learning. If the speaker is going to do a lecture style presentation which is longer than 15–20 minutes then it should be broken down into reasonable time slots allowing students to ask questions or make comments on what they have heard and seen so far. This means the teacher needs to prime the students and get them to have pre-prepared questions ready as well as asking spontaneous questions on the day.

Organising a guest speaker's visit often takes a great deal of time and effort particularly if they need access to audio visual equipment or specialist resources to do a demonstration. The teacher should also build activities around the visiting speaker's presentation so it is not seen in isolation to the rest of the topic. Such activities might range from having a discussion to the students doing an assignment or large cross curriculum project on a theme such as 'The Water Cycle'. Inviting a speaker from the local Water Company before the project starts to explain where water comes from, how we use it and how is it recycled, can stimulate interest and motivate the students into wanting to find out and learn more about our planet and its environmental issues.

## UNIT 2:  FACILITATING ACTIVE LEARNING

This Unit is about the teacher facilitating active learning. To learn effectively teachers need to design activities that get learners to do things, think about what they have been doing, make 'connections' with existing learning to develop new learning, and finally then apply their new learning. Once again this brings us back to Kolb's learning cycle and as a reminder it is illustrated in Figure 30.

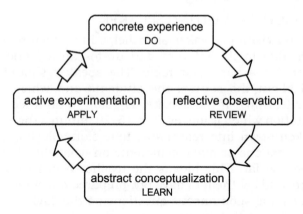

**Figure 30**: *Kolb's learning cycle – a participation model of learning*

This participative model of learning contrasts sharply with the traditional passive model of learning where learners are simply seen as just the receivers of information. Research clearly indicates learners will improve their learning enormously when they are required to take part in tasks that promote active learning. We hope the following illustrations will help and guide you to facilitate more effective active learning in your future practice.

## ACTIVITY A – GUIDING AND COACHING AN INDIVIDUAL LEARNER

When assessing learners' needs a teacher often encounters a student who has poor literacy and/or numeracy skills. Selecting this option gives, for example, a teacher in a craft workshop skills lesson on measurement and marking out an opportunity to demonstrate how they would guide and coach an individual learner to help improve their literacy/numeracy skills using practical activities. They would need to evidence how, through careful planning, the student is given sufficient 1:1 support in the lesson to help develop these skills whilst ensuring other members of the class are still fully engaged in learning. Similar examples can be evidenced in most practical workshops or laboratories where an individual learner is given appropriate guidance and coaching during, more often than not, a group activity. Liaison between subject teachers is crucial when supporting a student with learning difficulties and the days of saying to a student 'It's a maths problem so wait until your next lesson for the maths teacher to sort it out' we hope are long gone.

A problem all teachers face is how to guide and coach an individual learner who has missed some essential learning through illness or absence. Many institutions have now developed intranet sites so students can access learning materials from home via the Internet. The communication technology often enables the teacher to give 1:1 guidance and coaching specific to the needs of the individual learner. If such technology is not available an alternative approach could be for 'learning workshops' to be made available to all students who have missed essential learning or for those that want further support with a particular topic or concept. What the teacher needs to demonstrate in this activity is how they have devised active learning materials to help the individual learn. Ideally the learning materials are differentiated so the learner starts off with a task at which they experience success. The tasks then gradually increase in difficulty to extend their learning. The use of games, flash cards or computer simulations are some examples of active learning methods the teacher may develop to support this type of learning.

## ACTIVITY B — GIVING FEEDBACK TO LEARNERS AFTER ASSESSMENT

One approach that can be used when adopting this activity is for the candidate to evidence how a series of formative assessments, with feedback, has supported and developed students' learning. A technique now commonly used by many teachers is called the 'traffic light' system. What this means is that shortly after students start their course, usually within the first four to six weeks, they complete at least one or more formative assessments. This needs careful planning by the course team to ensure students are not overloaded with assessments at any one time. Each subject teacher then makes a decision based on the feedback from formative assessments as to whether a student is at 'green', which means they are coping with the work and should be successful; or at 'amber', which means there are some concerns in one or more of the subject areas but with more support they will eventually achieve; or at 'red', where it is recognised they will need a great deal of further support to be successful. This review takes place every six to eight weeks to ensure all students are progressing and will achieve when it comes to doing the summative assessments.

One way of putting the traffic light or any other learner feedback system into place is by using what Petty (2004: pp. 65-67) calls a 'Medals' and Missions' approach which was discussed in Section 1 (page 39). Remember a 'medal' is feedback that informs the learner about what they have done well such as *'Your predicted outcomes of global warming were well written and argued'* or *'The calculation to find the amount of power generated by the turbine was logically worked through'*. A 'mission' is feedback to the student about what they need to improve, correct, or work on. It is best when it is forward looking and positive such as *'Try to show all the important stages in your calculations'* or *'Your paragraph formatting is not clear. Refer back to the writing section of your class notebook and use it to re-paragraph this piece of work. This will help to make future written articles easier to read and understand'* . It is important to remember that grades and marks are measurements and many teachers are now giving formative assessment feedback only consisting of medal and mission statements.

## ACTIVITY C — HELPING SHY LEARNERS WITH CLASS INVOLVEMENT

Some students are shy and reluctant to participate in active learning methods such as group work, role play or discussions. The use of ice-breaking activities at the start of a course often helps learners start to overcome any shyness. The ice-breaking activities do not necessarily have to be anything to do with the course being studied but act more as a team bonding exercise to help students get to know each other. It is at this stage the teacher, if not already aware, can identify learners who may be shy and reluctant to participate in later planned activities.

A simple ice-breaking activity is to pair students up and get them to interview each other asking their name, interests, favourite TV programmes, etc. The roles are then reversed and each student tells the whole class about the person they have interviewed. A more vocationally related ice-breaker is to get the students to work in small groups to do some research and make a presentation on a well known writer, poet, artist, or scientist who has made a valuable contribution to society. All the students must participate in the presentation to some degree. The balance between helping a group of students to get to know each other and causing embarrassment is a delicate one. In any ice-breaking activity the teacher needs to exercise care and judgement so that no student feels threatened.

Another simple technique in helping shy learners with class involvement is the use of effective question and answer technique. Most experienced teachers use a great deal of questioning but it is the skill of how they use it that can engage all of the learners rather than just the vociferous few. Asking open ended questions and then giving the learners time to think is vital. Do not expect the answer immediately. After giving some thinking time the teacher should then nominate a student to answer. This is where the teacher can engage a shy learner to feel more confident by nominating that student and in doing so feeling fairly confident they will give the correct answer. Without going overboard thank the student for the response and praise the correct answer. Sometimes it is good technique to nominate another student to respond before confirming if the answer is right or wrong. Another effective questioning technique to help shy learners participate is to insert the word 'might' into the question. So instead of asking *'What is the meaning of equality?'*, which infers a single answer known by the teacher, ask *'What might the meaning of equality be?'* which is inherently a more open question. No teacher should under-estimate the value of effective question and answer technique in helping shy learners become involved.

Shy learners can also be helped to become fully involved in active learning through the use of well planned and managed group work. The types of activities and selection of the groups is vital to ensure all learners are engaged in the lesson. There are hundreds of possible contexts in which group work can be used but those commonly used include projects, assignments, case studies and role play. One of the great advantages of using group work is that most learners can get to higher order learning skills much quicker than working independently. All learners, even the shy ones, need to develop group working skills as most people work as part of a team in the business and commercial world.

## ACTIVITY D — ASSESSING THE NEEDS OF NEW LEARNERS

One approach candidates might take when selecting this activity is to devise an induction programme to assess the needs of new learners. At the beginning of a course a teacher usually has a thorough knowledge and understanding of what the learners are required to learn, the content of the course/ learning programme, but probably little knowledge of the learners themselves or their individual learning needs.  The information a teacher might have about the learners includes their name, gender, age and existing qualifications, but this will not necessarily be of any great help to them in the planning process. So what information does the teacher need to plan for effective learning to take place? As part of the induction process the teacher can use a range of initial assessments to identify individual learners' needs which include:

- basic literacy and numeracy tests
- learning styles questionnaires such as VAK style or Honey & Mumford
- psychometric tests such Gardner's multiple intelligence tests or left/right brain
- ice-breakers.

The feedback and subsequent analysis of these assessments can help teachers to plan, as far as possible, to meet the needs of their learners by gaining some insight into the following questions:

- How would they like to learn?
- Which methods in their previous learning experience have they liked best?

- Are learners' levels of physical, social and/or emotional development likely to affect their learning?
- What learning progress have they already made?
- What have they already achieved?
- Which skills are they confident in?
- What is their current level of knowledge and understanding?
- Which skills and/or knowledge might need to be revisited and/or upgraded?
- Do they have specialist needs in terms of health, disability, diet, language?
- What are their aims for education, long term career aspirations and life goals?

It is important that if learning styles questionnaires and psychometric tests are going to be used to assess learners' needs the students are not subsequently 'labelled' as being visual, kinaesthetic or auditory learners, or predominantly left rather than right brain, etc. Recent research indicates that most of these 'initial assessments' are not valid and extremely unreliable so should be used with the utmost caution.

It is important to devise activities within the induction programme that gives a teacher an insight into how learners' needs are influenced by factors such as gender, motivation, age, parental encouragement, levels of confidence and any language barriers if learners are using their second language. It is also misleading to think that a teacher can plan every session to meet the individual needs of every learner in their class; they can't unless they are teaching a very small class. This is why it is important teachers use a wide variety of teaching and learning strategies throughout the duration of the programme.

## ACTIVITY E — GROUP WORK

The range of group work activities and tasks is very wide. A few will be discussed here.

### 1. Single tasks

Groups are asked to carry out a task or series of tasks such as: *'Design and build a model of a house that our ancestors lived in 500 years ago; measure the velocity of an object every second from 0–10 seconds and then plot the results graphically to determine its acceleration and distance covered; use the library to research infant mortality rates from the year 1800 to the year 2000.'* Single tasks can also be set for individual as well as group work to stretch the more able learners.

## 2. Menu tasks

A menu task is where identical tasks are set and completed by all the groups or each group can select a task from a list of options. For example, all the groups could be asked to research and identify the main manufacturing industries of India. Alternatively each group could select from a list a region of India and be asked to identify the main manufacturing industries within that region. They would then be required to report back their findings to the whole class. Again, where possible the tasks should be differentiated so that if a group completes the task early they are required to do some further research on a more open-ended activity such as explaining why those particular industries were developed in that region. In some circumstances and when appropriate this type of group work can be made into a competition which is something students often enjoy.

## 3. Round robin tasks

This strategy requires the teacher to plan a set of tasks carried out by each group but in a different order. This means that at any one time each group is doing a different task but by the end of the 'round robin' all the groups have completed all the tasks. This group strategy is commonly used in practical situations where full class sets of learning materials or resources are not readily available such as in practical craft workshops, science and computer laboratories or specialist equipment workshops.

## 4. Buzz groups tasks

It is important when using this technique to have students working in groups of no more than four people and to break down the topic to be discussed into manageable tasks with appropriate time constraints. For example, if buzz groups were formed to discuss how paper is made and its uses, ideally this activity would be broken down into a number of tasks such as:

➤ identify six different uses of paper
➤ name four different sizes of paper and where they are used in the home or office
➤ identify materials paper is made from.

Buzz groups can be used in many situations to promote active learning. If a teacher has to give a presentation or demonstration then it can be interspersed with buzz group activity. Teachers also often use buzz groups to get students to answer questions when revising for summative examinations. The class layout must be conducive for buzz group discussion and the activities kept short, usually a maximum of five minutes.

## 5. Snowballing tasks

In this technique the teacher initially puts students in pairs to complete a task such as discussing an issue or solving a problem. Pairs are then combined to make groups of four who compare answers to the first task and complete a related task. If necessary groups of four can be combined to make groups of eight but there is a danger that some students may not engage in the learning when working in such large groups.

An example of snowballing is to give pairs of students a short paragraph to read which contains a number of grammatical errors which they must identify in five minutes. The pairs then go into groups of four and the students are given ten minutes to compare answers and discuss what needs to be done to correct the errors. For the last five minutes the groups of four are combined into groups of eight who compare and discuss the work they have done and agree on a correct solution.

## 6. Brainstorming or mind-showering tasks

Brainstorming is used when the students are required to create a number of ideas for subsequent evaluation. It is particularly useful when starting project or assignment work but can be adapted to most classroom/workshop learning situations when ideas or solutions to problems are required. Managing groups doing brainstorming activities can be difficult so clear ground rules must be set by the teacher and/or negotiated with the students.

At a simple level students could work in groups to brainstorm and come up with as many ideas as possible, no matter how unusual, as to what useful objects they could make from a one metre length of plastic tube and some string. When students are working on large projects such as designing and manufacturing a machine for crushing metal cans the brainstorming activities involve not only all the technical aspects of making the device but also the potential environmental impact.

### 7. Peer tutoring and peer checking tasks

In most group work activities there is always an element of peer tutoring taking place. When planned for, careful selection of the groups needs to be made by the teacher so all students benefit from the activity. Most games and activities where students are developing higher cognitive skills lend themselves to peer tutoring and peer checking.

A simple example of peer tutoring is where groups of students are given a set of flash cards and each card has a decimal number written on it which is less than 1 and the cards are in a random order eg: 0.75, 0.375, 0.04, 0.8, 0.125, 0.4, 0.25. The group must initially place the cards in descending order. The more able students will be able to explain to the less able why 0.375 is smaller than 0.6, which is a common misconception with many students. After placing all the cards in order the teacher then gets each group to check another group's answers. To extend the activity the groups are then asked to place in descending order another set of randomly ordered flash cards with the proper fractions $^3/_8$, $^4/_5$, $^1/_8$, $^3/_4$, $^2/_5$, $^1/_4$, $^1/_{25}$. The students are not told that each fractional value corresponds with the decimal values which, through peer checking, are already in the correct descending order. Again the more able students can help the less able to see and establish the relationship between the decimal and fractional numbers as well as explaining how to convert a fraction to a decimal and a decimal to a fraction. This type of differentiated activity covers all levels of Bloom's Taxonomy from knowledge through to evaluation and lends itself to peer tutoring and checking tasks.

## ACTIVITY F — DEVELOPING LEARNER ICT SKILLS

It is doubtful if any discipline does not utilise some aspect of ICT and it is now integral in most if not all learning programmes. Therefore this activity has a wide range of possibilities, no matter what subject is being taught, to develop learner ICT skills through active learning. The approach for this activity should be for the teacher initially to identify what learner ICT skills need to be developed and then devise suitable activities to develop those skills. Many teachers think of developing a learner's ICT skills as simply getting the student to sit at a computer on an individual basis and operate some software, with the teacher giving support as and when required. This would be a mistake. If you are a non-specialist ICT teacher it may be useful to consult with specialists to discuss ways in which they use whole group, small group and individual learning strategies to develop their learners' ICT skills.

One approach a candidate might take for this activity is to develop her/his students' presentation skills using ICT as most people are now required to do this as part of their job. Initially the teacher might involve the whole class by discussing what makes a good presentation which concludes with the students agreeing to a checklist or rubric that can be used to evaluate presentation skills. The class is then organised into buzz groups to identify and then analyse the advantages and disadvantages of using different types of ICT presentation software and each group reports back their findings. Finally each student must then prepare and do a two minute presentation on an agreed topic where their peers give feedback and assess it using the checklist.

It is often a fact of life that no matter how young the learner they often have far more ICT skills than the teacher. This is particularly the case when using the Internet as a 'learning' resource. However, this is not the same as developing a student's research skills which involves a wide range of abilities, including the use of ICT, and needs careful planning and development by the teacher. Students could initially be set directed tasks on a small group or individual basis to search for specific information from websites to support their learning such as finding the main naturally occurring resources of a region in India or the birthplace and dates of important historical figures such as Mahatma Gandhi or Albert Einstein. Alongside this they would also have to find the same information from the library as it is often a much more efficient way of accessing information when carrying out a 'closed' search. Once familiar with the type of resources the teacher wants them to find, students can then be given the responsibility of doing their own searches to research a particular topic, it's surprising what they come up with!

What the teacher must focus on when using this approach is to develop the learners' ICT skills, not their own. The teacher might use free internet software to create crosswords or multiple choice quizzes but what they could do is get the students to use the software to create these fun activities and then use them as part of the learning programme. Not only does this type of activity develop higher order thinking skills but it promotes active learning.

## UNIT 3: REFLECTING ON PRACTICE

In this unit the chosen activity focuses on ways and means teachers develop their thinking and critical awareness of the practice of teaching and training. The activity requires the teacher to reflect and evaluate a professional development experience away from the immediate learning environment. It is worth reminding candidates that the Certificate for Teachers and Trainers uses Kolb's learning cycle as a 'model' for learning and reflection is seen as an essential part of that process.

## EXPERIENCE A — PLANNING A SCHEME OF ASSESSMENT

Teachers use a scheme of work to plan a series of lessons to achieve the course aims in the most effective way. In doing so they attempt to provide students with as wide a variety of activities to meet their learning needs as possible. The same approach can be used when planning a scheme of assessment, which can either be built into a scheme of work or produced separately.

The scheme of assessment will include both formative (ongoing) and summative (final) assessment methods which as a reminder can be used to:

- measure the relationship between the objectives and the learners' learning
- monitor the progress of learners' learning
- highlight strengths or diagnose the learners learning weaknesses
- provide feedback to learners leading to future improvement
- provide feedback to teachers and other stakeholders
- select learners for courses, subjects of study or employment
- predict future achievements
- estimate learners' current skills
- form part of a learner's profile of abilities
- contribute to some publicly recognised accreditation system
- recognise prior achievement and experience
- demonstrate to learners they have attained some goal or acquired some skill
- motivating learners to learn.

If, as is more than likely, a teacher prepares a series of formative assessments culminating in one or more summative assessments, they could do this as part of the approach used for Unit 1 and the activity selected for Unit 2. Alternatively it could be developed as an independent experience. What's important is that, as with Units 1 and 2, teachers 'experiment' and are prepared to 'take risks' when developing a scheme of assessment. There are a wide range of methods that can be used for both formative and summative assessments, it does not always have to be a traditional short answer or essay activity. The list below is not exhaustive but does indicate the variety of possibilities:

- short answer questions
- long answer questions
- essays
- objective (multi-choice) tests
- oral questioning
- producing creative arts and artefacts
- assignments – problem-solving tasks
- observation
- role play
- portfolios
- diaries and log books
- projects and reports
- computer-based assessments.

If teachers are teaching lower ability groups they need to develop assessment methods that mainly test the students' knowledge, comprehension and application and not their memory skills. Having a good memory is seldom part of the assessment criteria so why are students penalised when they can't remember a scientific or mathematical formula to answer a question? Here is an opportunity to demonstrate how valid and reliable assessment questions can be constructed so as not to disadvantage such students. Students who have difficulty in expressing themselves in writing are also often at a disadvantage. This is where methods such as objective (multi-choice), oral and computer-based tests can be developed that assess the student's required learning and not their writing skills.

To fully evaluate any scheme of assessment the teacher needs not only to develop, administer and mark assessments but also to provide feedback to the learners, as this is an important part of the assessment process. Gibbs and Simpson (2004) indicate that out of the 11 conditions under which assessment supports learning, 7 of them are based on feedback. Black and Wiliam (1998) spent four years researching the links between formative assessment and feedback and they stress that:

> *Feedback has extraordinarily large and consistent positive effects on learning compared with other aspects of teaching or other interventions designed to improve learning.*

The participants required to give feedback when selecting this experience will be the learners and a professional observer. Candidates should also be using a reflective journal or diary to record events, thoughts, feelings, etc as the experience develops such that it can be used for their reflective practice.

## EXPERIENCE B — PLANNING AND MANAGING A MEETING FOR TEACHERS/TRAINERS

Most if not all programmes of study require teachers to participate in regular course team meetings to review individual student and course progress. If a candidate has never organised such a meeting this may be a good opportunity to do so. As with any meeting to address a specific purpose or activity there needs to be clear aims and objectives along with a plan to ensure the aims and objectives are met.

A candidate might want to organise a meeting with teaching colleagues to discuss and share experiences from the approach adopted in Unit 1 and/or the activity used in Unit 2, and the impact this has had on students' learning. Whilst most teachers are familiar with receiving observer feedback from managers and peers they might want to discuss what the experience has been like obtaining feedback about teaching and learning from their learners and how did the learners themselves feel about it. Sharing and reflecting on such experiences can be very beneficial to all concerned.

Other scenarios a teacher might consider to plan and manage a meeting include:

- making changes to a syllabus
- introducing a new programme or individual subject of study
- using some new ICT software, internet sites or equipment to support learning
- using some new educational technology such as interactive whiteboards.

The possibilities for this activity are numerous as so much of a teacher's time is spent on doing things outside the classroom. However, as with Units 1 and 2, feedback is required from the participants involved in the experience such as colleagues, managers and a professional observer.

## EXPERIENCE C — RECORD KEEPING

A great deal of a teacher's time is now spent on administrative tasks and for this experience the candidate is required to devise a new way of keeping, using and storing records. The following list is not exhaustive but does demonstrate the wide variety of records kept by teachers, methods used for storing them and possibilities of how they can be used.

1. **Formative assessment results**

   Many courses are now unitised and the results from each unit's formative assessment results could be kept and maintained on a spreadsheet. If correctly set up this could enable all teaching staff to have access to the spreadsheet so they can see at a glance the learning progress of an individual student, not only in the subject they teach, but in all other subjects. If a 'traffic light' system is introduced to monitor individual student learning then the spreadsheet could automatically flag up the 'at risk' students at any time.

2. **Summative assessment questions and result**

   With unitised courses it is important that teachers and students can monitor learning achievement at any time throughout the course. If a course comprises of 18 units studied over two years, and in each unit there is a average of six continuous summative assessments, this means each student will require up to 108 summative assessment records! If an individual student's progress is not monitored until near the end of the programme, by that time it is usually too late to rectify the situation and they may have potentially failed the whole course. A 'traffic light' system to record all summative assessment results could be developed to maintain and keep records so they are regularly monitored and readily available to teachers, students, employers, parents and external awarding bodies as and when required.

The recording and analysis of previous external summative assessment questions is another technique teachers sometimes use to prepare students for exams. If formative assessment feedback indicates a student has particular areas of weakness or gaps in their learning the teacher can take questions from a resources 'bank' to support their learning.

### 3. Learners' individual learning plans

Many teachers are now required to keep and maintain a learning plan for each individual student. If this is the case and no useful pro forma already exists a candidate could devise an individual learning plan that can be used by the course team, department or across the whole establishment. If one already exists they could re-design it so any information can be uploaded directly onto a computer for easy access, retrieval and analysis.

### 4. Course self-assessment reports

As part of an institution's quality assurance procedures many teachers now have to produce an annual course self-assessment report. The self-assessment report contains data that enables the analysis of trends such as learner retention and achievement over the past three to five years. The results can then be benchmarked against national or known averages. The report may also comment on more qualitative aspects of the course such as:

➤ identifying learners' individual needs

➤ quality of teaching and learning through lesson observation

➤ in-course learner support

➤ course leadership and management.

A candidate who has responsibilities for a course or programme of study may use this opportunity to devise ways of keeping records as part of a management information system against which judgements about the quality of the provision can be made.

## EXPERIENCE D — PASTORAL CARE AND ADVICE

All teachers have a duty of care towards their students, no matter what their age, and they need to acknowledge that all learners have their own individual problems. Therefore it is crucial teachers establish a climate of mutual respect and rapport so students are able to approach them with any personal problems or difficulties that may impact on the learning process. However, when using the experience of pastoral care and advice for the activity in Unit 3 it is important it is undertaken only with the help of appropriately trained specialist colleagues. There are also issues of confidentiality to be considered whether providing pastoral care and advice to an individual student or a group of learners.

A teacher might decide to use their recent experience of providing pastoral care and advice to an individual as a case study where a student has been supported emotionally and/or financially to overcome personal problems that have allowed her/him to continue with their studies. The candidate could link back to Unit 1 if they have provided support to a student with problems associated with an educational visit or participating in role play. Supporting an individual could also potentially be linked to most of the activities listed in Unit 2.

Most young students now participate in PSHE (Personal, Social, Health and Economic) programmes of study that focus on their personal and economic well-being. For this experience a teacher might start to get involved in different aspects of a PSHE education programme such as:

- identifying PSHE learning opportunities across the curriculum
- preparing and/or delivering specific PSHE lessons to a class
- preparing and/or delivering specific PSHE whole school activities
- preparing information, support and guidance on specific areas of PSHE learning
- identifying PSHE learning opportunities through involvement in the life of the school and the wider community.

PSHE education is most effective when it uses a wide variety of active learning and assessment approaches and provides frequent opportunities for children and young people to reflect on their own and other people's experiences so they can use and apply their learning in their own lives. Active involvement in the life of the school and wider community should help young people recognise and manage risk and take increasing responsibility for themselves and their choices.

The aim of PSHE education to equip children and young people with knowledge, understanding, attitudes and practical skills to live healthy, safe, productive, fulfilled, capable and responsible lives is still valid in further, higher and adult education. Programmes of study at these levels could incorporate aspects of PSHE education such as encouraging learners to be enterprising and supporting them in making career choices and managing their finances effectively. It will also enable them to reflect on and clarify their own values and attitudes and explore the complex and sometimes conflicting range of values and attitudes they encounter now and in the future. In this context a teacher could devise a programme that could be used by any department and then adapted to suit a particular subject or vocational discipline. Where possible, any issue should also be used to develop a core skill such as literacy or numeracy. Students could use their numeracy skills to calculate the amount of salt in their daily diet and compare it with what is recommended for healthy living. Similarly they could research the number of calories in their favourite foods and then calculate how much exercise they would need to do to burn off those calories.

If selecting this activity candidates might need to be reminded that feedback for review and evaluation must still be obtained from a professional observer who may be a teaching colleague or specialist such as a counsellor or student advisor. Feedback also needs to be obtained from the participants who could be teaching colleagues, an individual student, or a group of students, and this process must be managed sensitively.

## EXPERIENCE E — MAKING A PRESENTATION TO A LARGE GROUP

The choice for this experience is enormous as it can be on any educational subject the teacher selects. Therefore it is important they establish clear aims and objectives as it could include not just sharing how a new teaching approach was developed in Unit 1, or active learning was facilitated in Unit 2, but the development of the candidate's own presentation skills when presenting to a large group.

Large groups are usually considered as consisting of twenty plus participants. However, this does not mean the teacher has to give a lecture style presentation. They may decide to take a more active and interactional approach to achieve their aims and objectives. The target audience for developing this professional experience is groups of teaching staff, parents, employers or other outside bodies.

A candidate may decide to make a presentation to a group of colleagues on how they approached planning and managing an interesting and successful educational visit they feel would be of interest to all. This could then be used as a forum for sharing ideas about how to make the best use of educational visits to develop student learning.

Organising a presentation to a group of parents could also be based on the theme of organising an educational visit and how the teacher would like their involvement and support to make the activities successful. To generate enthusiasm the teacher could incorporate into the presentation a slideshow or some video/DVD footage from past educational visits.

Teachers are also now marketeers. A candidate could make a presentation to a group of parents of prospective students outlining the range of courses the institution offers, the resources used to support learning and the pastoral care and support available. Organising an awards ceremony to celebrate student success could be another experience a candidate might develop with a target audience that could include parents and representatives from a range of outside bodies.

As well as the professional observer, a candidate also needs to obtain feedback for review and evaluation purposes from the participants. Designing an evaluation questionnaire to be completed immediately after the presentation or at a later date is one way of obtaining this information. Alternatively the candidate could allow the participants time for reflection and then organise some focus groups to obtain relevant feedback.

## EXPERIENCE F — WORKING WITH ANOTHER DEPARTMENT

In many institutions staff from different departments seldom interact and share ideas about new approaches to teaching and learning. This is a good opportunity for a teacher to work with a colleague from another department to trial and share ideas about how to develop more active learning methods. Using this approach may involve shared lesson observations where the recorded feedback can be used as part of the review and evaluation process. Most teachers find it is much more productive and enjoyable to work with colleagues to help generate ideas and learn, just as their own students do.

In the industrial and commercial world professionals often work on projects with a wide range of people from different disciplines so one approach a teacher might take is to work with a colleague from another department to develop a joint project. For example, students from different disciplines could be asked to work together to design, test and make a simple product prototype that can be used in the home, garden, nursery, playground, beauty salon, etc. As part of the project students would be required to make a presentation and a competition could be organised to judge the best product against agreed criteria.

A candidate might work collaboratively with another department to purchase some new equipment such as an interactive whiteboard and then develop their ICT skills in how to use the resource effectively. They can then, as part of a staff development programme, organise and deliver training in their own and other departments to support and improve teachers' presentation skills. Another approach might be for a candidate to work with colleagues from other departments to research and develop an ICT central resource bank to support teaching and learning across all disciplines.

Working with a mentor who can act as the professional observer might be useful if this experience is selected for this Unit. Designing an evaluation questionnaire or organising focus groups to obtain feedback for review purposes also needs to be carefully thought through so judgements can be made to evaluate if the experience aims and objectives have been met.

# SECTION 6

## REFLECTIONS AND OPPORTUNITIES

Reflections and Opportunities

# REFLECTIONS AND OPPORTUNITIES

In some senses we should begin thinking about the Kolb teaching-learning cycle with its fourth stage 'Evaluation'. This book may have given you ideas about your own professional situation and how it affects the development of the ways in which your learners learn. So our final chapter seeks to help you with your own reflection and the ways forward from such considerations.

## ON REFLECTION

Whether or not you have completed the Certificate it is always a good idea to take stock of your own professional practice for the mid and longer term. This is rather different to the more immediate on-going and end of module or course evaluations which we carry out during the school or college year. Here we are looking at evaluation of our own professional practice rather than evaluation of learning sessions or learning programmes. Some may see this as merely 'navel gazing' and others may see it as a rather selfish activity. Neither assertion has much merit. As teachers, our pedagogical work very often casts us in an advisory, sometimes counselling role. We would be better placed to help others with their ways forward if we thought about our own.

The first reflective thought many professional people have concerns success and failure. This is understandable since many societies link promotion and to some extent, pay to indicators of success. As we have already seen, the pressure to help learners gain the best possible grades has tended to promote results in tests and examinations as by far the most important evidence for evaluation. This has tended to affect teaching-learning methods, funnelling them into practices characterised as 'spoon feeding'. This in turn casts doubts upon the value of the educational process as a whole and there has been some back-pedalling on the necessity for quite so much mass assessment – in the United Kingdom, for example.

We would only say that to see your own professional practice solely or even primarily in such assessment based terms would do you as a teacher and certainly your learners rather an injustice. Your reflections should be framed in other terms beside 'success and failure'. For example you may have implemented a new learning programme which might involve learners in fresh learning experiences. Our Unit 1 in the Certificate lists six ways in which this might arise but there are many other areas for development in the curriculum. It might be that you have played a part in setting up a new system of pastoral care. You might have set up a properly indexed school library or set up exchange visits to other schools. The effects of these cannot be measured by assessments such as examinations but they may well have a more significant long term effect on the ways in which learners benefit from learning.

Evaluation works best if you write down your thoughts and your reflections on your professional practice and collect evidence from your own notes, the reflections of your learners, discussions with colleagues (including appraisal), reports from inspectors and points made by parents. Of course, we can add the results of internal and external assessments of your learners. Once you can see the whole picture then you can write out what needs to be remedied or improved.

Both writers were involved in appraisal processes in a school or college context. Appraisal is an incomplete (and sometimes rather negative) process if it dwells upon solving problems, bemoaning inadequacies of resourcing and not much beyond. Surprisingly few appraisal candidates have worked out what they would like to do professionally even in the short term. Almost none have written their aspirations down. Perhaps it just needs an injection of positive thought, so our next section helps you to look at ways forward.

POSSIBLE WAYS FORWARD

In Figure 31 we have represented the teacher as a turtle enjoying a nice swim in the warm sea of evaluation! Why a turtle? Well, here is a well-travelled creature, liked by many and yet with a well developed carapace which helps it endure 'the slings and arrows of outrageous fortune'. It is a good, happy image to begin our sequence of ideas. And you will see that we have used our turtle motif to focus our thoughts on some ideas for future professional development which you might like to consider in the light of the following sections which expand on the five possibilities shown on Figure 31.

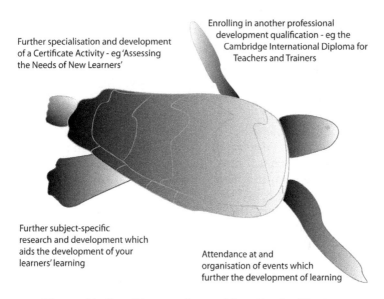

Some possible ways forward from the Certificate

Further specialisation and development of a Certificate Activity - eg 'Assessing the Needs of New Learners'

Enrolling in another professional development qualification - eg the Cambridge International Diploma for Teachers and Trainers

Further subject-specific research and development which aids the development of your learners' learning

Attendance at and organisation of events which further the development of learning

**Figure 31**: *Possible ways forward from the Certificate*

## 1. Further development of a Certificate Activity

It may be that in undertaking a Certificate Activity you have become particularly interested in its content and application and would like to develop it further. For example, most schools and colleges have procedures for admitting learners to the institution and that involves some sort of induction. This is a very important matter for all concerned – learners, teachers and parents. Very often administrative and organisational needs are satisfactorily dealt with but what of learner needs? As teachers we know that the quicker we make ourselves familiar with the needs of our learners the better able we are to provide Learning Programmes and Learning Sessions which meet those needs. How might we best facilitate the acquisition of such knowledge? There are many methods including:

➢ diagnostic tests in subjects like Mathematics and Languages
➢ reference to prior learning from the records of previous teachers
➢ questionnaires on preferred learning styles
➢ subject specific interviews.

These are fine and very useful if handled in a sensitive fashion given that newcomers to a school or college are likely to be nervous or apprehensive. Many teachers have found that they can learn a great deal from less formal activities which form part of an induction programme such as role play, practical work, team work exercises and so on. Very important and often ignored is gaining an idea of learner interests, aptitudes and aspirations. These can be seen in terms of skill preferences and confidence in terms of those skills. Too often learners are addressed as 'customers' responding to 'tick boxes' rather than individuals with a very distinctive set of characteristics which may well produce extraordinary learning. The issue in induction is to keep asking questions of learners in a friendly and approachable way and make a record of what you discover. How you design this and put it into action in your own professional context is of course a matter for you and your colleagues and that could well be developed through further study.

## 2. Enrolling in another professional development qualification

If you have enjoyed being involved in Certificate study you might be interested in moving on to big sister qualification – the Cambridge International Diploma for Teachers and Trainers. The Diploma features four modules – Design, Practice, Assessment and Evaluation – and shares a common conceptual underpinning with the Certificate.

Perhaps you have become really interested in the application of ICT to the development of learning; we have referred to this many times in this book (especially when considering Unit 1 Approach B and Unit 2 Activity F. Very much worth considering in this context is the Diploma's twin qualification, the Cambridge International Diploma in Teaching with ICT. Both qualifications are supported by a range of support and stimulus materials and you can access syllabus and other details on the CIE website www.cie.org.uk

### 3. Enrolling in further academic qualification

CIE professional development qualifications are essentially practice-based and call upon theory as and when applicable. It may be that you feel a need to return to academic studies either in the context of your subject specialism or in Education itself. This usually takes the form of undertaking a Master's degree on a full-time or part-time basis. Clearly there is a vast range of these available and the reader is urged to make enquiries locally and/or on the Internet to see what exactly is available. Never be afraid of being a 'mature learner' – their ranks are swelling as courses multiply and become more easily accessible through e-learning.

### 4. Events which further the development of learning

These range from large-scale international conferences such as those organised by CIE to more local conventions, exhibitions and meetings. Again the Internet, professional organisations and institutions of Higher Education are excellent sources of information and point the way towards rewarding involvement and teacher development and you might even be able to take some of your learners along. Education is very much a sharing as well as caring professional world and it is increasingly international. Both writers would encourage readers to make use of such 'events'. You will meet lots of other teachers and who knows what opportunities will unfold. If there is nothing much happening in your area or region, why not form a development group with other local teachers and organise a programme yourself?

## 5. Further subject-specific research and development

All CIE professional development qualifications are designed to be 'generic' – that is they can be based on practice in any part of the world, at any learner 'level' and in any subject-specialist domain. It may well be that reading books like this whets your appetite to develop specialist learner knowledge, understanding and skills. CIE organises specialist training courses for teachers, especially in conjunction with IGCSE and A level but increasingly also with primary education and other age groups as the Cambridge International Curriculum develops. The focus of all these is learning and learners.

Other springboards for further study include national subject professional organisations and their regional branches. Very often national and provincial education authorities have details of contact addresses and websites. There are yet further opportunities in examining and inspection. These may seem remote from the day-to-day learning context but it is surprising how much even quite detailed ideas on practice and assessment you can pick up through involvement in such activities. Some countries such as Singapore offer teachers the opportunity to work in areas such as curriculum development and assessment before moving back into teaching after a number of years. It may also be possible to apply for research sponsorships and scholarships in your own country or elsewhere.

# APPENDICES

## APPENDIX 1

MEMORY TEST 1

Place a sheet of paper covering rows A to J. Move the sheet of paper down so that row A is revealed. Read aloud the four numbers and then cover up Row A and see if you can remember all four. If you are successful move onto Row B which has five numbers and then row C which has six. How far can you get before you reach the data capacity of your conscious mind?

| | | | | | | | | | | | | |
|------|---|---|---|---|---|---|---|---|---|---|---|---|
| Row A | 5 | 1 | 7 | 9 | | | | | | | | |
| Row B | 6 | 3 | 0 | 5 | 2 | | | | | | | |
| Row C | 1 | 5 | 3 | 0 | 4 | 5 | | | | | | |
| Row D | 5 | 9 | 6 | 1 | 0 | 2 | 3 | | | | | |
| Row E | 2 | 1 | 4 | 2 | 6 | 3 | 8 | 4 | | | | |
| Row F | 7 | 9 | 1 | 6 | 3 | 8 | 6 | 1 | 3 | | | |
| Row G | 1 | 6 | 3 | 2 | 4 | 8 | 6 | 4 | 8 | 0 | | |
| Row H | 6 | 8 | 9 | 1 | 6 | 2 | 0 | 7 | 9 | 5 | 9 | |
| Row I | 1 | 3 | 2 | 6 | 3 | 9 | 5 | 2 | 6 | 5 | 7 | 8 |
| Row J | 0 | 9 | 1 | 8 | 2 | 7 | 3 | 6 | 4 | 5 | 5 | 4 | 6 |

MEMORY TEST 2

Now try this activity. Row A has six digits grouped together as three pairs, each pair forming a number. Read aloud the three numbers in Row A i.e. 'fifteen' 'thirty' and 'forty five'. Now cover up the row and see if you can remember the three numbers. If you can, try Row B and so on.

| | | | | | | | |
|------|----|----|----|----|----|----|----|
| Row A | 15 | 30 | 45 | | | | |
| Row B | 21 | 42 | 63 | 84 | | | |
| Row C | 16 | 32 | 48 | 64 | 80 | | |
| Row D | 13 | 26 | 39 | 52 | 65 | 78 | |
| Row E | 9 | 18 | 27 | 36 | 45 | 54 | 65 |
| Row F | 21 | 28 | 35 | 43 | 48 | 56 | 63 |

MEMORY TEST 3

Now study the following nine symbols over the page *for* thirty seconds then cover the information up and see how many letter symbol pairings you can remember.

1 = ⌋     2 = ⎩⎭     3 = ⌊     4 = ⎤     5 = ☐

6 = ⌈     7 = ⌉     8 = ⌈⌉     9 = ⌈

Now try to represent the same information in a different way so it is more easily absorbed and retained (hint – think of a 3 x 3 square reading from the top left corner as number 1 to the bottom right corner as number 9).

## APPENDIX 2

AIMS AND OBJECTIVES 'TEST'

The answers to the activity identify aims (A) and objectives (O) are shown below.

| | | | |
|---|---|---|---|
| 1 | know the difference between an aim and an objective | A | |
| 2 | translate a selection of French menus' into English | | O |
| 3 | prepare, cook and present for service a two-egg plain omelette | | O |
| 4 | understand the principles and methods of assessment | A | |
| 5 | list, in order, the health and safety procedure for someone who has had an electric shock | | O |
| 6 | draw a colour wheel using the four primary colours | | O |
| 7 | develop skills in writing business letters | A | |
| 8 | appreciate the problems of world pollution | A | |
| 9 | place data from other files into the correct place in a document | | O |
| 10 | write, in legible handwriting, a 1500 word essay on the theory of memory in learning | | O |
| 11 | know the operation of an internal combustion engine | A | |
| 12 | solve a quadratic equation using more than one method | | O |

# APPENDIX 3

LESSON OBSERVATION CHECKLIST – TEACHER FOCUSED

| **1. Planning and preparing the session – the teacher:** | Yes | No |
|---|---|---|
| • produced a coherent and logically sequenced scheme of work | ☐ | ☐ |
| • produced a lesson plan with clear learning objectives/outcomes for the session | ☐ | ☐ |
| • produced a lesson plan with a clear structure – beginning, middle and end | ☐ | ☐ |
| • had a clear view of the learners' needs and capabilities, or a plan to find out | ☐ | ☐ |
| • selected a range of learning activities to promote active learning | ☐ | ☐ |
| • designed the lesson to elicit and sustain students' attention, interest and involvement | ☐ | ☐ |
| • prepared suitable resources and learning aids to support learning | ☐ | ☐ |
| • set up the room and facilities with attention to all health and safety considerations | ☐ | ☐ |
| • arrived on time to create a warm learning environment | ☐ | ☐ |

| **2. Opening the session – the teacher:** | Yes | No |
|---|---|---|
| • shared the learning objectives with the students | ☐ | ☐ |
| • outlined the plan of the session to the students | ☐ | ☐ |
| • started the lesson by linking back to previous learning | ☐ | ☐ |
| • checked the present level of students' knowledge, skills and understanding | ☐ | ☐ |
| • dealt appropriately with late-comers | ☐ | ☐ |
| • dealt appropriately with unprepared students | ☐ | ☐ |
| • re-negotiated the session if necessary | ☐ | ☐ |
| • linked the session with students' previous experiences and interests | ☐ | ☐ |

### 3. Teaching and learning methods – the teacher:      Yes  No

- selected methods appropriate for the students' age and abilities  ☐ ☐
- selected methods appropriate for the subject matter being taught  ☐ ☐
- used a variety of methods that promoted active learning  ☐ ☐
- selected methods that made the students use higher order thinking skills  ☐ ☐
- motivated the students by being enthusiastic and making the lesson interesting  ☐ ☐

### 4. Presenting material – the teacher:      Yes  No

- structured learning materials to give students early success and stretch able learners  ☐ ☐
- used language appropriate for both the subject matter and ability of students  ☐ ☐
- emphasized and continually reinforced key learning points  ☐ ☐
- used appropriate pace for the exposition of learning material and information  ☐ ☐
- checked on a regular basis that presented material had been understood  ☐ ☐
- made presentations and demonstrations lively and interesting  ☐ ☐
- evidenced up-to-date subject knowledge and skills  ☐ ☐
- ensured tone of voice was clear and modulated for variety and emphasis  ☐ ☐

### 5. Supporting students – the teacher:      Yes  No

- distributed attention fairly among the students
- used appropriate verbal and non-verbal communication to motivate the students  ☐ ☐
- supported students, regardless of ability, on an individual and small group basis  ☐ ☐
- responded appropriately to equal opportunities issues  ☐ ☐
- was aware of what was going on elsewhere while working with an individual student  ☐ ☐
- promoted students' own problem-solving and independent learning skills  ☐ ☐

- dealt with any difficult or challenging students consistently and effectively ☐ ☐
- set clear boundaries and maintained class discipline at all times ☐ ☐

## 6. Using activities and exercises – the teacher:                **Yes  No**

- selected activities and tasks that fully engaged the learners' interest ☐ ☐
- selected activities that contributed to meeting session objectives ☐ ☐
- briefed everyone clearly so students knew what was expected from them and when ☐ ☐
- timed changes of activities to maintain student interest ☐ ☐
- structured activities to give all students early success ☐ ☐
- set challenging tasks for the more able students ☐ ☐
- designed activities that promoted group work ☐ ☐
- pitched any intervention at the most effective level ☐ ☐
- made use of the results of the activities to modify the rest of the session ☐ ☐

## 7. Using resources – the teacher:                             **Yes  No**

- selected and prepared resources appropriately (quality of handouts, OHTs, etc.) ☐ ☐
- demonstrated good techniques of using resources (board skills, use of OHP, etc.) ☐ ☐
- used Information Communication Technology appropriately to support learning ☐ ☐
- ensured the resources used did not disadvantage any students ☐ ☐
- used appropriate resources for all cultural groups ☐ ☐
- produced good quality learning materials and handouts for future reference ☐ ☐

## 8. Relating to students – the teacher:                        **Yes  No**

- created a welcoming learning atmosphere and maintained a suitable working culture ☐ ☐
- ensured all the students were involved in the lesson ☐ ☐
- responded constructively to students' questions and comments ☐ ☐

- communicated interest and enthusiasm for the subject ☐ ☐
- responded appropriately to students' 'off-task' activities ☐ ☐
- helped all students to feel their contributions were
  valuable and valued ☐ ☐
- gave frequent praise and encouragement to all learners
  for effort and progress ☐ ☐

### 9. Promoting active learning – the teacher:                 Yes   No

- created opportunities for students to take responsibility
  for their own learning ☐ ☐
- created opportunities for students to learn from each
  other ☐ ☐
- ensured the students felt they had a contribution to
  make to the learning process ☐ ☐
- ensured the students were learning at the appropriate
  level (Bloom, etc.) ☐ ☐

### 10. Managing the session – the teacher:                     Yes   No

- managed to fit the work into the time allocated ☐ ☐
- allocated time according to session priorities ☐ ☐
- managed a smooth transition between activities ☐ ☐
- ensured the students knew what they should be doing
  at all times ☐ ☐
- made good use of unexpected happenings ☐ ☐

### 11. Assessing learning — the teacher:                       Yes   No

- used open questions to continually check students
  understanding ☐ ☐
- gave the learners thinking time when answering
  questions ☐ ☐
- ensured it was not always the same people answering
  questions ☐ ☐
- responded constructively to incorrect responses and
  did not answer own questions ☐ ☐
- used a range of formative assessments to check
  knowledge and understanding ☐ ☐
- maintained records of assessment results to monitor
  students' progress ☐ ☐

- gave students opportunities to assess their own work and progress ☐ ☐
- used assessment results to identify gaps in students' learning ☐ ☐
- gave positive and constructive critical feedback on student work ☐ ☐

## 12. Concluding the session – the teacher:   **Yes  No**

- ensured the session had a clear conclusion summarising the learning ☐ ☐
- assessed what has been learned ☐ ☐
- made links with the next session ☐ ☐
- set clear expectations if work is set between sessions ☐ ☐

## 13. Evaluating the session – the teacher:   **Yes  No**

- knows if the learning objectives have been met and how ☐ ☐
- knows what was done that ought not to have been done ☐ ☐
- knows what was left undone that ought to have been done ☐ ☐
- knows what should be done differently next time ☐ ☐
- knows what to do the same next time ☐ ☐
- knows what else the students learned, apart from what was set out to teach them ☐ ☐
- involved the students, formally or informally, in evaluating the lesson ☐ ☐

The list of questions under each heading is not exhaustive and could be added to or condensed. What is evident is that the range of knowledge and skills a teacher needs to plan and deliver a successful lesson is substantial. However, even if the answer to all the observation questions is 'yes', do we really know that all the students have learnt what they are supposed to have learnt, as the focus of each question is predominantly on the teacher and not the learning?

The next checklist does put the focus on the learners and their learning. It could be used in conjunction with the teacher checklist so subsequent feedback focuses on both learning and teaching.

# APPENDIX 4

## LESSON OBSERVATION CHECKLIST – LEARNER FOCUSED

| Lesson observation checklist – focus on the learners | Yes | No |
| --- | :-: | :-: |
| • turned up on time and quickly settled down to work | ☐ | ☐ |
| • found the learning activities motivating and their interest was maintained throughout | ☐ | ☐ |
| • made suitable progress in the learning activities to achieve all the learning objectives | ☐ | ☐ |
| • participated in activities that challenged all of them, including the more able learners | ☐ | ☐ |
| • demonstrated through positive body language they enjoyed the lesson | ☐ | ☐ |
| • made relevant contributions, asked questions, offered ideas, etc | ☐ | ☐ |
| • showed a keen interest in the activities and tasks they participated in | ☐ | ☐ |
| • took pride in their work | ☐ | ☐ |
| • understood concepts and could explain what they were doing and why | ☐ | ☐ |
| • interacted productively as they were learning | ☐ | ☐ |
| • demonstrated interest in the subject and were engaged throughout the lesson | ☐ | ☐ |
| • participated in a variety of activities and kept on task | ☐ | ☐ |
| • undertook activities that enabled them to develop and then apply knowledge and skills | ☐ | ☐ |
| • participated in activities that required deep thinking and were challenging | ☐ | ☐ |
| • had their work in progress checked and corrected | ☐ | ☐ |
| • received praise/rewards for effort, progress, completion of tasks etc | ☐ | ☐ |
| • received criticism that was constructive to help them achieve | ☐ | ☐ |
| • received support when it was required to successfully complete tasks | ☐ | ☐ |
| • took responsibility for their own learning and were motivated to learn | ☐ | ☐ |

- had opportunities to work in pairs or groups and to support each other ☐ ☐
- had opportunities to take control, exercise initiative, and make individual responses ☐ ☐
- demonstrated their achievements through improved knowledge, understanding and skills ☐ ☐
- were engaged in activities suitable for all, whatever their age, ability or experience ☐ ☐
- found the learning activities demanding for the range of abilities within the class ☐ ☐
- provided regular feedback to the teacher on their learning and progress ☐ ☐

# BIBLIOGRAPHY

Abbott, J. (1994) *Learning makes sense: Recreating Education for a Changing Future*, Education 2000

Amabile, T. M. (1999) 'How to kill creativity' in *Harvard Business Review* on Breakthrough Thinking, Harvard Business School Press

Ashcroft, K. and Foreman-Peck, L. (1994: 54) *Managing Teaching and Learning in Further and Higher Education*, Falmer Press

Atherton, J. S. (2005) *Learning and Teaching: Bloom's taxonomy* [Online] UK: Available: http://www.learningandteaching.info/learning/bloomtax.htm
Accessed: 17 April 2009

Beadle, P. (2005) 'Red all over: Thorough marking of a student's work can cement a special creative relationship', The Guardian, Tuesday 10 May 2005

Black, P. & Wiliam, D (1998) *Inside the black box: Raising standards through classroom assessment*, King's College London

Bloom, B. S. (1965) *Taxonomy of Educational Objectives*, Longman

Bloom, B. S. (1956) *Taxonomy of Educational Objectives: The Classification of Educational Goals*, Susan Fauer Company, Inc., pp. 201–07

Borger, R. and Seaborne, A. (1966) *The Psychology of Learning*, Penguin

Broadbent, D. (1958) *Perception and Communication*, Pergamon Press

Coffield, F. (2008) *Just suppose teaching and learning became the first priority....* Learning and Skills Network

Gardener, H. (1993) *Creating Minds*, Basic Books

Gibbs, G. and Simpson, C. (2004) 'Conditions under which assessment supports student learning', Learning and Teaching in Higher Education 1, pp.3-31

Hattie, J. (1999) Influences on student learning
Available: http://www.geoffpetty.com/downloads/WORD/Influences onstudent2C683.pdf Accessed: 4 April 2009

Knowles, M. et al. (1984) *Andragogy in Action: Applying modern principles of adult education*, Jossey-Bass

Kolb, D. (1984) *Experiential Learning: Experience as the Source of Learning and Development*, Englewood Cliffs, NJ: Prentice Hall

Maslow, A. H. (1987) *Motivation and Personality*, 3rd edn, Harper & Row

Petty, G. (2004) *Teaching Today: A Practical Guide, 3rd edition*, Stanley Thornes

Petty, G. (2009) *www.geoffpetty.com/downloads/WORD/constructivism3.doc*
Available: http://www.geoffpetty.com Accessed: 23 April 2009

Petty, G. (2009) *Improve your teaching... and that of your team*
Available: http://www.geoffpetty.com Accessed: 23 May 2009

Petty, G. (2009) *www.geoffpetty.com/*
Available: http://www.geoffpetty.com Accessed: 29 June 2009

Pickett, N and Dodge, B (2009) Rubrics for Web Lessons, Accessed 13 May 2009 at http://webquest.sdsu.edu/rubrics/weblessons.htm

Race, P. (2005) *Making Learning Happen: A Guide for Post-Compulsory Education*, Sage Publications

Race, P. (1993) Never Mind the Teaching, Feel the Learning, SEDA Paper 80, 1993
Accessed 5 May 2009 at http://www.londonmet.ac.uk/deliberations/seda-publications/race.cfm

Reece, I. and Walker, S. (2003) *Teaching, Training and Learning: A practical guide*, 5th edn, Business Education Publishers Limited

Schön, D. (1983) *The Reflective Practitioner: How Professionals Think in Action*, Basic Books

## FURTHER READING

Amabile, T. 'How to kill creativity', *Harvard Business Review* (March 3, 2009)

Belbin, M. http://www.belbin.com/

Bruner, J. (1986) *Actual Minds, Possible Worlds*, Harvard University Press

Dweck, C. S. (2006) *Mindset: The New Psychology of Success*, Random House

Gardner, H. (2006) *Changing Minds: The Art and Science of Changing Our Own and Other People's Minds (Leadership for the Common Good)*, Harvard Business School Press

Kyriacou, C. (1998) *Essential teaching skills*, 2nd edn, Nelson Thornes Ltd.

Petty, G. (2004) *Teaching Today*, Nelson Thornes Ltd.

Race, P. (2005) *Making Learning Happen: A Guide for Post-Compulsory Education*, Sage Publications

Shaw, S. and Hawes, T. (1998) *Effective Teaching and Learning in the Primary Classroom: A practical guide to brain compatible learning,* Optimal Learning

Van Der Veer, R. (ed), Valsiner, J. (ed) (1994) *The Vygotsky Reader,* Wiley-Blackwell, Oxford

## Some useful websites

Cambridge International Examinations website www.cie.org.uk

### Active learning

http://www.geoffpetty.com/activelearning.html

http://tlp.excellencegateway.org.uk/resource/su_ict_introrescd/activelearning/whatis.htm

http://www.teachers.tv/video/32322

### Assessment for Learning

http://www.qca.org.uk/qca_4336.aspx

http://www.teachers.tv/video/2864

### Lesson observation and feedback

http://www.teachers.tv/video/1517

### Bloom's Taxonomy

http://www.teacherstoolbox.co.uk/blooms_taxonomy.html

### Evaluating teaching and learning

http://golddust.bdplearning.com/assessment_for_learning/evaluating_teaching_and_learning.php

### Learning – constructivism

http://www.teacherstoolbox.co.uk/constructivism.html

### Learning and motivation

http://www.youtube.com/watch?v=r-wD3M59Uiw

http://www.teacherstoolbox.co.uk/Dweck_Motivation.html

http://www.teacherstoolbox.co.uk/maslow.html